Lady,

Apurva Purohit is the President of the Jagran Group, one of India's largest multimedia conglomerates. Amongst the very few women CEOs in India, she has over three decades of experience in building and scaling up high-quality businesses in the private equity and listed space. Apurva has been ranked as one of the Top 30 Most Powerful Women in Business as per *Business Today* 2016 and 2018, as well as *Fortune India's* Most Powerful Women in Business 2018.

She is also the author of the national bestseller *Lady, You're Not a Man!* Apurva is an ardent advocate of gender diversity in the workplace and seeks to embolden and encourage women to reach their full potential through her books, mentorship and lecture series. She is a post-graduate from IIM-Bangalore.

You can connect with Apurva at:
www.apurvapurohit.com
www.twitter.com/apurva_purohit
www.linkedin.com/in/apurva-purohit
www.facebook.com/womenatworkin

Lady, You're the Boss!

Apurva Purohit

First published by Westland Publications Private Limited in 2019

1st Floor, A Block, East Wing, Plot No. 40, SP Infocity, Dr MGR Salai, Perungudi, Kandanchavadi, Chennai 600096

Westland and the Westland logo are the trademarks of Westland Publications Private Limited, or its affiliates.

Copyright © Apurva Purohit, 2019

ISBN: 9789388754415

Typeset by SÜRYA

To
My mother – Asha Kanwar
Sanjay and Siddharth

Contents

Prologue

'**M**a'am, *how* did you know this is the *exact same* problem I've been having with my husband?' young Neha excitedly quizzed me, getting her grammar all muddled up in her enthusiasm. She had just finished reading *Lady, You're Not a Man!* and got in touch with me virtually the moment she put down the book. 'It seems as if you were in the room with us while we were arguing!' she said. 'How did you know that I don't want to leave my child with my mother-in-law? You can't imagine how badly she has brought up my husband!' she whispered. Laughing, I told Neha that no, I hadn't peeked into her bedroom specifically. I certainly didn't have a third eye embedded into my forehead nor could I lay claim to soothsaying abilities, much as I would like to. The simple truth was that her story was the story of every young woman I had met in the thirty years of my career. And her call was neither the first phone call I had received attesting to that fact, nor would it be the last!

Lady, You're Not a Man! discussed issues that all working women have faced at some point or the other in our lives – from being guilt-ridden when our young children ask us not to go to work, to being convinced by our mothers/in-laws that staying at home after marriage is the right thing to do because after all, 'God has given us everything, so why on earth would we need a second income?' as if that is the only reason we want to work! The book took a peek into our bedrooms and boardrooms and pointed out how all of us had equally lazy husbands or difficult bosses and suggested ways of dealing with these troublesome, albeit lovable, beings in our lives as we went along our merry adventures at work.

I have witnessed so many women sacrificing their careers because they were not clear about their priorities and were accepting the status quo, or because they were not asking for help, or because they mistakenly believed that in the give and take of being a woman in a man's world, they could only partially achieve their dreams. I wrote *Lady, You're Not a Man!* to tell these young women that they could have it all too, because the distinction between women who have succeeded and those who have not, is actually not so much about aptitude and talent, but attitude and perseverance.

Like Neha, many of you wrote to tell me that it made you laugh when you figured out the 'you too?' moments and I believe several of you felt deeply consoled that your problems were not uniquely your own. You told me that the book had empowered you to become the heroine of your story and had provided several useful suggestions, which you had used to improve your lives.

However, as my conversation with all of you deepened, I realised that it was still incomplete. Without a doubt, many of you have done well in life and successfully found the balance between home and work. You are paddling your way pluckily through the turbulent waters of gender-agnostic environments. But somewhere in a little corner of your heart, you have also succumbed to the belief that there is a ceiling beyond which you cannot grow. After all, only 17 per cent of start-ups have a woman partner, just 5 per cent of senior-management roles in organisations are filled by women, and only 3 per cent of VC funding goes to women entrepreneurs. There are hardly any women in public spheres like politics or policymaking and even fewer women university chancellors and IIM directors.

Many of you, while having stable careers and being individually brilliant, have reconciled yourselves to being defined only as Sonu's mom or Vivek's wife. And these are the things you and I need to change.

I have met you in different personas: as businesswomen, professors, scientists, tarot-card readers, editors or corporate managers. And I have seen loneliness in your eyes. With whom do you share the particular tribulations that come attached to being a working woman? The stress over getting the next promotion or not getting it? The frustration in dealing with a male subordinate who thinks he should have been the boss instead of you or the investor who looks at you and not your male partner while asking for a cup of coffee?

You may not have met them but there are many valiant women exactly like you, fighting tough battles in the big bad world all by themselves. Under all our different skins and varying skin-tones, we are soul sisters dealing with precisely the same issues. Whether apple-shaped, pear-shaped or an hourglass type, at the core we are ultimately identical – a mix of confidence and self-doubt that makes us single-handedly take on the world one day, and a bundle of nerves the next. And I want to share the anecdotes of your sisters with you, so you recognise that this is not your battle alone and draw strength and succour from their stories.

It is a fact that even today despite their stellar achievements, women are still treated as second-class citizens of the world. Whether getting talked over at board meetings (or at home) or not getting funding for a start-up as brilliant as any man's or just not getting paid as much as male colleagues, there seems to be a cosmic endeavour to ensure that women remain firmly seated on the substitutes' bench and never get to play the match.

There is no doubt in my mind that many external prejudices and stereotypes are obstructing your path to glory. However, I believe that there are several mistakes you are making too, which are preventing you from achieving the peak of what you are capable of.

It bothers me to see that you still lack confidence and continue to have the tentativeness of a young novice, despite all those certificates of excellence on the wall behind you. It concerns me that you have become fed up of fighting for your rights incessantly and have thus decided to give up on the battle. I watch as you adjudicate poorly on your own behalf by downplaying yourself and minimising your abilities. As a result you are fulfilling a mere fraction of your true potential.

I know that there is an entire universe inside you, waiting to be discovered, but I see you sitting at the edge of your seat, always afraid that someone may throw you out of the room because you believe that you are an imposter who will get caught one day despite your accomplishments.

But here's the truth: unlike Cinderella, you are not going to turn back into a beggar-maid at the stroke of midnight. You have genuinely worked hard to reach here. You rode to the ball not in a carriage conjured out of thin air by a fairy godmother, but in the car you bought with your own hard-earned money.

You did not need a fairy godmother to get you this far, but you do need someone to tell you that you definitely deserve to be here! And that there are vast and unconquered opportunities still ahead of you. Because the one single unassailable truth is that your best version is yet to come.

For that to happen however, there is only one magic wand and it is firmly in your own hand – when you realise that only you can prevent yourself from being condensed or minimised.

The world with its inherent patriarchal order will wish to lock us inside a narrow box of mores and traditions. But we cannot and must not allow it to bonsai us. The glass ceiling, whether of our own or someone else's making, has to be shattered.

In my own journey, it took a long time to understand this and most of these wise thoughts came to me around the age of fifty, when finally I became truly confident about who I am and when menopausal changes, while playing havoc with my sleep pattern and metabolism, were also ensuring higher testosterone levels and thus higher degrees of aggression. Behaviourally I have inevitably been a late bloomer (what can I say?) and, I feel I could have done many things differently if only I had that extra dose of gumption earlier. But there is no reason at all for you to have to wait for that testosterone to kick in!

When you read this book, you will realise that it invites you to reflect on what you have achieved so far, the restrictions you have imposed on yourself and how you have many times swayed to a tune not of your own making, by adjusting and accommodating, by choosing to keep quiet and by allowing yourself to drift. As you reflect, I hope you will recognise that the time has come for you to decide for yourself what you want to do and that this time around, you get to choose what you want. Just remember that your prospects are limitless and infinite, and they will take you wherever you want to go.

Rumi, the patron saint of the Twitteratti, says: 'Are you a drop in the ocean or the ocean in the drop?' *Lady, You are the Boss!* is for women who believe that no boundaries should curb them, no shackles should bind them and no barriers should come in the way of what they can truly achieve.

I hope this book gives you the courage to dance to a tune of your own making and pushes you to the furthest limits of your potential in your adventures at work.

PART ONE

A Minimum Life?

He says you are too much. You talk, laugh, smile, feel too much.
But baby, here is the real problem. He is too little to
appreciate that it took an entire galaxy being woven
into one soul to make you.

—Nikita Gill

Centuries ago our cave-dwelling ancestors began a pattern of behaviour that seems to be continuing to this day in workplaces across the world.

In those days, men had to go out to hunt while women stayed in their caves to care for the children and the elderly and thus each behaved in a way that aided them best in their respective roles. The men donned masks and body paint, puffed up their chests, yelled battle cries and made themselves larger than life to intimidate their prey. The women, sharing a small living space with so many others, shrank themselves as much as they could to cooperate with each other and to avoid communal strife.

Thousands of years of evolution later, many things have changed. For example, men and women alike leave their homes to earn a living. But some things have not. The brunt of the care for children and the elderly is still shouldered by women. But the most puzzling unchanged status quo is that men still don their metaphorical war paint and puff up their chests with aplomb while women continue to shrink themselves to take up as little space as possible, despite the fact that they are going a-hunting too!

A male sales head will confidently proclaim that he has achieved his target even if the reality is that he has barely scrambled past the 80 per cent goalpost! A company of five hundred employees becomes a thousand and a two-crore salary becomes four when the story is being told by a lad! A fellow just about competent to be a marketing head will declare himself entirely ready to be a CEO. And I am yet to come across the CV of any Indian male in which he hasn't asserted that he was the captain of his university cricket team and always was a topper to boot!

All is bluff and bluster (and par for the course) in the day of a macho corporate Zorro. After all, even Antonio Banderas wore a mask. However, this doesn't bother me much since I have learnt to moderate any grandiloquent statements the gentlemen around me make. So if HD* (husband dearest) says he will be back by nine, my mental clock auto-corrects it to 11 p.m. If one of my CEOs says, 'Don't worry boss, we will deliver the goods within forty-five days at 100 per cent quality,' I immediately make mental notes to tell our clients that seventy-three days is the earliest they can expect the shipment. And when my male friends tell me that they had the most amazing holiday in the most beautiful villa on the hippest island in the Aegean Sea, where they had perfect weather throughout the third week of October, you can be sure that except for the fact that they did go on vacation, nothing else is remotely accurate!

---

*You may remember him from *Lady, You're Not a Man!*

What worries me however, is that women too have not evolved significantly from their cave-dwelling selves! They have been shrinking and subduing themselves from time immemorial and continue to operate at sub-par visibility levels even in contemporary times.

We brush aside compliments, don't speak up, speak hesitantly when we do, never ask for raises, negotiate superbly on behalf of others but never for ourselves, and let others take credit for our work. Despite being given a senior role or promotion based on merit, we continue to behave as if we don't actually deserve to be there and deem that the roles of sales head, CEO, managing partner or principal are way above our station!

Sadly, it is not just our cave-dwelling ancestors who should be blamed for our public mousiness. It is also the way we have been brought up and are bringing up our daughters – by censoring and diminishing them to be lesser than they are. We train our daughters to take up as little space as possible – not laugh aloud or dress flamboyantly or do anything that draws attention. We do it for their sake, to protect them, but unintentionally and wretchedly end up teaching them that to be invisible is good for them. Then how can we expect them to behave differently when they grow up?

When my yoga teacher sternly reprimanded me for the nth time about my poor posture, I flashed her a guilty look and sighed in frustration. I had hoped these weekly classes would be an escape from the madness of work. But the teacher's constant, albeit well-meaning, prods about my hunched shoulders were making me feel like a slightly feeble-minded pupil!

She had tried correcting me patiently. But the moment

I took my attention off them, my stubborn shoulders hunched forward of their own volition.

How could I explain to her that I may be a confident CEO in my fifties, but to my overprotective shoulders, I was still the confused little girl trying to deflect the attention of the creepy local uncle, even though I didn't understand what he was looking at! I was still the timid adolescent girl navigating a crowded street. I was the young adult trying not to get groped on the bus. It is an instinct honed by girls across the nation to avoid attracting the wrong kind of notice. Almost from our childhood, we learnt to hide our bodies using books, clipboards and every object from quotidian life, which could pass for armour; we intentionally developed a poor posture and walked with our heads down hoping this would be enough to keep us from being pawed. We dressed down, spoke softly and walked as tentatively as we could, moving about cautiously in a world that didn't want us to occupy too much space in it.

When my yoga teacher glares at me for not getting my posture right, how do I tell her that fifty years of self-protective instincts do not evaporate overnight no matter how hard I try?

Both evolutionarily and behaviourally, the cards are frustratingly stacked against women. Men on the contrary have always been taught to maximise themselves. Whilst women shrink, slink, crouch and refrain from taking up too much space, men naturally move into it and claim it as their own.

A glaring example of this is the predominantly masculine noises we hear all around us – inside our homes; on our television screens; in public places, institutes and offices.

When I go to women-only colleges for workshops, all the students are vocal and boisterous. Certainly there are differences among those who speak up and those who don't, but that is largely attributable to differences in personality types. Bolder girls speak up and confidently express themselves, expecting to be heard – and that is a beautiful sight to behold. Quite a different experience awaits me when conducting workshops in co-ed colleges. There are no introverts and extroverts anymore. Only women and men! Invariably, the shy participants hanging back are women and the confident talkers asking questions are men!

Across classrooms and boardrooms, this pattern reveals itself without fail. In common spaces, women automatically register societal cues that designate them as second-class citizens, and lo and behold, they dissolve into secondary and silent characters.

In my own case I notice that although I have an important point to make in a board meeting, I hesitate. I avoid interrupting whoever is talking, which leaves me with limited occasions to talk, since the other board members, obviously male, are incessantly and continuously talking. I feel guilty if I take an extra minute to voice my opinion, because the board schedule has a time-bound agenda. My fellow board members, all male, are gloriously oblivious to any such dilemma as they interject at will, speak with utmost confidence about subject matters they are least qualified to have an opinion on, and drone on and on even as the poor company secretary starts fidgeting and looking agonisedly at the ticking clock.

And when I do find a pause in the proceedings (which only happens when said board members have been distracted by the arrival of tea, coffee and cookies) and muster up the courage to speak, I am likely to say, 'I have just a small point to make ...' or 'May I only specify ...' or 'Umm, maybe this is not the right way to evaluate competition.'

Just? Only? Maybe? Such pallid, insipid language! I know the points I am making are of significance, I know that nobody else in the room has arrived at these inferences. But evidently my tongue doesn't know this and continues using vocabulary that is destined to be snubbed.

It is no wonder that my fellow directors started taking me seriously only after several board meetings and repeated exposure to my inputs. It was not their fault; they were all very intelligent and thoughtful human beings. But if my own tone was hesitant, my body language timid and my words diffident, why would anyone have the patience to analyse the content when time was a constraint?

We think our work will speak for itself, good deeds will always be noticed, talent will not remain hidden for long, so we choose to keep quiet, either deliberately or because we have been conditioned to do so. I want to break your heart right here and tell you this is complete and utter moonshine, like the fairy tales we read in our childhood.

In order to be recognised, appreciated and successful, you have to be your own fairy godmother and your own advocate. And you had better hurry up because the boys who have read the same fairy tales were being programmed to go out, slay the dragon and blow their trumpets from the grandstands.

The only way to deal with this tentativeness is to stand up boldly, make your voice heard and your opinion matter. Like Kirti, a friend of mine. A famous author and well-known Twitter influencer, Kirti was called out by a mutual friend for promoting her books on Twitter. Our friend said this was rather forward of her. Kirti was unapologetic. 'Who will promote my books, if not me?' she asserted. And rightly so. If we don't talk about ourselves, I assure you no one else will.

If our voices are not heard and we are not forceful in our articulation, how will our opinions register in an uncaring and dismissive world? By being visible and vocal in private and public domains, we add our voices to the chorus that forms opinions and becomes the basis for any action. The wisdom of the crowd always prevails, and if we want pro-women actions, it is up to us to ensure we are a significant voice in that crowd.

We may live in a world that trains us into silence. But fortunately, we live in times when we know not to take such instructions silently. To begin with, let us fight strong, talk loud, laugh hard and assert ourselves without guilt. Let us take up as much space as we want, stand tall and walk upright with pride. Let us live unabashedly, loudly and wholeheartedly.

A life lived in fear is an abbreviated, feeble life. And that life is not for you, a woman who has the whole universe residing within her!

IN SHORT

- Women have been conditioned over centuries to minimise themselves.
- This reflects in their behaviour at work too, where despite being competent they are far more tentative, unsure and diffident than they need to be.
- We need to change this and the change can only come from within, when we reclaim our voices and proclaim our talent and skills to the world, loudly and unapologetically.
- If men can be their own publicists, what stops women from doing the same? After all we are competing in the same domain.
- Let's change how we bring up our daughters. Let us allow them to be as boisterous, flamboyant and visible as our sons. They deserve the same amount of space as their brothers.

Imposter Syndrome

I have a self to recover, a queen. Is she dead, is she sleeping?
Where has she been, with her lion-red body, her wings of glass?

—Sylvia Plath

I stared at our new head of HR with some consternation. She stared back, perplexed. The fact that she was highly competent was not under debate. Her terrific track record and dynamic thinking had led to her being appointed the head of the department at an age much younger than the norm. But as I sat there, trying to have a conversation with her that I'd repeatedly had before, I realised with a sinking feeling that she was not her predecessor.

Her predecessor, Sara, had been an aggressive and assertive department head who hadn't much cared for boundaries. She had unerringly understood the implicit authority of her role and therefore had been involved in the functions of all the other departments. She saw herself adding value to those departments and would make sure that she was not only part of the decision-making, but also an active influence there. Through intelligent use of her abilities and experience she had expanded the parameters of her role so well that HR was treated as a crucial voice at the boardroom table and not merely as a support department in the organisation.

When it was time for Sara to move to a higher position, I was sad to lose her. But I recognised that a person of her calibre needed a playing field proportional to her ever-expanding skillset. Enter the new recruit – our young but talented HOD from whom we expected great things.

Janice came into the organisation at a time when we were going through a huge sales challenge. But she made no move to pitch solutions or offer opinions about it. As we sat having this now-familiar conversation, I asked her why she wasn't a part of the sales meetings.

'I wasn't invited,' she replied glumly.

'I hope you realise that revenue is currently our biggest challenge? What's the concept of HR that we have built in this organisation? It's not just to recruit and train people. It's also to be involved in the business functions and see how you can be a source of support. Your role is exactly the same as that of your predecessor. You are supposed to be a partner to the CEO. Are you seeing yourself like that or not?' I asked, frustrated.

Janice looked like she desperately wanted to please but didn't know how. As she gazed at me deeply anguished, I felt like I had kicked a puppy. Truth be told, I identified with her more than she realised. And I was hard on her because I saw her on the verge of making the same mistake I had once made. With disastrous consequences.

I am talking about a mistake many women make repeatedly, a self-debilitating misconception they suffer from called, rather dramatically, 'The Imposter Syndrome'. The syndrome is defined as a psychological pattern in which individuals doubt their accomplishments and internalise their fears of being worthless. They feel that their position has been handed to them by a twist of fate or good fortune and that they have not earned it. This leads them to be tentative and uncertain, exactly when they are supposed to be pushing themselves to make the most of a new opportunity.

Flashback to three decades ago when I was a bright-eyed twenty-something who had only one goal in life – to get into an IIM. While appearing for the Common Admission Test, an exam that about two lakh entrants take and only two thousand crack, I was not nervous. I was a bright student. I had been preparing for it with single-minded focus and had aced all the practice tests.

When the results came in, no one was surprised to learn that I was the only person from my batch to have got through to IIM Bangalore, Ahmedabad and Kolkata at that first written stage. But the interview round was quite another matter. The conservative home environment I grew up in deemed all knowledge that was not in the school syllabus irrelevant. My inherent shyness didn't help matters. I performed poorly in the group discussion and interview rounds.

When the results were announced, I was shattered to find that I hadn't made it to any of the IIMs. My family went into mourning. I spent the next few months moping over broken dreams, staring forlornly every morning at our letterbox and willing the unlikely call letter to drop into it. And then one day, magically, it did.

This was their second list. I hadn't made it on their first. I couldn't care less. I packed my bags and rode off into the sunset. Given how precious this victory was to me, I worked hard to make the most of it. The first two months at IIM, I did well in every new subject that was introduced. Even the alien finance and quantitative mathematics courses were no match for my voracious determination.

Then as I slowly started getting to know my classmates better, I learnt that the majority of them were from IIT and had some impressive work experience under their belts. I started comparing myself with all the bright sparks around me and suddenly the fact that I hadn't made it on the first list took on new meaning. It must be because I was a mere graduate from a regular college with no work experience! That was who I was – a second-lister who had meandered by sheer luck into a constellation she was never supposed to be part of! I spent the next few weeks walking around with scarlet letters of shame plastered figuratively on my forehead!

And then the obvious happened. My grades started to dip and for the remainder of my first year, I did poorly in all my exams. The eight to nine months of failure were wrapped in not only misery but also mystery. How did I lose the plot so badly?

I was hurtling full speed in a downward spiral and I could not pull the brakes. From the shame of not being a first-lister to not being as qualified as my classmates, I let externalities convince me that I was not good enough. Imposter syndrome tells you you're a fraud for choosing to inhabit the role you've rightfully earned. Back then, I believed it.

Many years after this IIM debacle, a previous boss asked me to head Zee TV. The job would be a quantum leap from my then-current position. Hesitantly I accepted. The environment I entered was a highly charged one. Amid rampant internal workplace politics and intense external competition from the newly re-launched Star Plus channel, it was a time of crisis. Three months later, the CEO who got me into the organisation left it. Isolated in that unfriendly atmosphere, with my only source of support gone, I began to question my ability to get the job done. The ground was ripe for the imposter syndrome to raise its ugly head yet again! 'I am not trained for this job.' 'This position is higher than the promotion that would have come about in the normal course of my career.' 'This malevolent environment is just not conducive to productivity.'

But this time I was better prepared to handle these invidious beliefs, simply because I knew they were lurking like ghostly shadows around me.

I reminded myself that nobody was questioning my qualifications to be there except myself. Outwardly everyone was seeing the president of Zee TV even if inwardly I felt like a junior executive starting her first job. I knew I could help that organisation. I knew that my ex-manager had not recommended me for this position as a favour. The stakes were much too high for that. He had done so because he felt I was the most qualified person for this task.

Backing my own intelligence and reinforcing my sense of self-worth to myself, I realised, were the key to fighting the deadly insidious forces of imposter syndrome. This time around, I was committed to becoming my own ally instead of a saboteur. And I proceeded to own my role as president and did work I am still proud of.

The syndrome shows its worst form when we are given a platform to operate on and we choose to occupy only a small part of it. Quite like my newly minted HR head was now doing. 'I am too young. I am too junior. The CEO and I are not at the same level. I can't barge into meetings I am not invited to.'

We all suffer from this syndrome at some point in our lives. Yes, even that confident alpha male colleague who is ponderously explaining the impact of agrarian distress on the economic environment to you just now!

And my own experience tells me that there is a deceptively simple way to fight this enemy. Self-talk. It works like magic but we just do not do enough of it. In this highly connected world we spend so much time having partial conversations with best friends, half best friends, enemies turned friends, mere acquaintances and random aliens that we forget the most important person we need to talk to – the person belonging to the face that stares at us every day in the mirror.

It is vitally important that we reacquaint ourselves with her, talk to her and remind her of all the hard work, perseverance and talent she has, that have brought her to this juncture. The successes she garnered in the past because of her ability and the impact she generated because of her skill are not a twist of fate. They are her right and her due.

Then we need to go back to repeating a basic exercise we learnt in elementary school – Match the Columns. The moment we start matching the column of our skills with the column of the tasks at hand, we will realise that there is no better person to do those tasks.

Who will stand up and fight for us but ourselves? Especially when the ghosts are inside and not outside us? We can do anything we want. We are capable. We are in this place because we've earned the right to be here. And if we have to fight with our own selves to believe that, then fight we must. The imposter is not you. It never was.

IN SHORT

- Women suffer from 'the imposter syndrome', which insidiously tells them that they are not good enough to be where they are and that it is just happenstance that aided their progress, not their experience or skills.
- They are reluctant to fully occupy the platform they have been given because of this belittling belief and end up compromising their growth.
- Constant self-assurance is the trick to chase out the imposter from within.
- It is crucial to accept that the world knows what it is doing when it presents women with opportunities, and they must make full use of the breaks they get.

Strengths Not Weaknesses

I take most things as a compliment.
I find it makes life much easier.

—Dowager Countess, *Downton Abbey*

From the comfortable distance of thirty-five years I can look back and laugh at my adolescent self. Poor thing, she seems to have spent her teenage years mostly being either tongue-tied and shy, or moody and angry. A large part of those painful years however, was spent being hopelessly mortified at everything around me – the old Fiat car my father drove breaking down at awkward intervals, entailing all of us getting out and pushing it when we were all dressed in our finery; my sister laughing loudly in movie halls; my parents going to meet my teachers at school; or me developing a football-sized stye on the day of my cousin's wedding!

It is a medical fact that teenagers suffer from something known as cognitive distortion as a result of the mismatch in the development of different parts of their brains as they are growing up. This distortion results in exaggerated and unreasonable thoughts that cause them to misperceive reality and then subsequently feel bad. Every small thing that goes wrong, such as a stye in the eye, is either a catastrophe of ginormous proportions or it is a personal attack on their self. (Why did fate make me look so ugly with one eye half-blinded because of that huge stye just on the day of the sangeet when there are so many good looking boys around and everyone else is looking so gorgeous? I am doomed forever!)

However, as teens grow into adulthood, the laggard part of the brain responsible for calm reasoning catches up with the fast-paced anxious part and things start falling into some semblance of peace and quiet. While this biological evolutionary theory seems to have explained everything very neatly and tied it up with a cute bow, it appears as if the female brain missed reading this, because it continues suffering from heightened anxious brain syndrome despite moving deep into adulthood! What else can explain our peculiar penchant for always seeing the negative in ourselves rather than the positives? For concentrating on criticisms rather than praise? For seeing all flaws magnified manifold in ourselves? And thus remaining acutely anxious most of the time?

Certainly I see a wide disparity in self-confidence between the male and female managers who've worked under me. A female manager will come out of a presentation and immediately start muttering about all the things she did wrong. She will filter out all the positives and retain only the mistakes she made. While the male manager usually swaggers out of such meetings assured that he's just delivered the Gettysburg Address. Recently we had one such incident. One of our male senior heads was supposed to talk about a specific topic. Instead he gave a long-winded speech that jumped from his childhood to Aristotle while meandering through an example about an extreme sport no one had heard of. It had little to do with the topic at hand

and, frankly, made little sense. He came up to me with a self-satisfied smirk after the meeting and drawled, 'That went rather well, no?'

I goggled and gasped and wiggled my eyebrows, which is my default response with these pompous lads, since banging them on the head with a hefty hammer could be misconstrued as unprofessionalism!

It would be hilarious if this were an isolated incident. But when the pattern keeps recurring without break, then the joke is on us women. Two friends of mine – Rajni and Rajeev – recently left their jobs to become entrepreneurs. Rajni has set up a digital platform that offers integrated wellness solutions to corporate employees. She has been working for the past twenty years in this field. She had researched extensively before embarking on the project. The technology that she is implementing in her start-up is highly innovative. But a year has passed since she began working on it and there is no launch date in sight.

Every time she comes to me for a mentoring session, she shares how she has changed the platform yet again, how she has tweaked the services on offer or how she has improved the website. But she continues to leave each session unsure of the viability of her project and even less ready to go public with it than she was at the beginning of the session.

Rajeev on the other hand launched his start-up in four short months. He created a digital platform that aggregates bookings and appointments for hotels and clubs. He has had as tumultuous a time of it as Rajni – getting side-tracked by false starts, having to change technology partners and dealing with a lot of pressure from investors in trying to get conversions.

But at least he started. And because he started, he's seeing some success. This, in turn, is helping him move forward. Whereas Rajni is floating about in a pool of her own uncertainty. Every time I meet Rajeev, he is on an entrepreneur's high. 'Hey, Apurva, this service is going to actually change the way we live our lives, it's a blockbuster! Everyone I meet says they have never seen such a platform,' he exclaims.

I envy his confidence. Here's a guy who is helping businesses manage their bookings and he is convinced he is changing the world because of it. Rajni's platform has the ability to genuinely improve people's lives and, consequently, the actual potential to make the world a better place. But her confidence is non-existent because she can only see the problems in her platform. Her insecurities are so strong that she may never get around to doing anything either for the world or for herself!

Focusing on and magnifying weaknesses is not the monopoly of women alone. I look around at what happens in our organisations and I see a flawed system at work. When creating our training programmes, we typically analyse the skills of all the people in the organisation and figure out their strengths and weaknesses. More often than not, training programmes concentrate on how to overcome those weaknesses while taking the strengths for granted.

Great sports teams are built on the opposite philosophy. Good coaches know that the secret to a knockout performance lies in building on a player's strengths and minimising their weaknesses. If Sachin Tendulkar was constantly told to improve his bowling, where would our cricket team have been? Why strive to be an average all-rounder when you can be the world's greatest batsman? When we leverage our strengths to tackle challenges we become the best version of ourselves.

A very long time ago I knew a girl who worked with me in advertising where she started her career as part of the batch of management trainees we got every year. As seniors, we trained them for six months before sending them out into the big, bad world. There's a reason she stands out in my memory even after so many years.

Tanya was a slip of a girl, about four foot nothing. Really tiny and from a no-name college. All of us seniors subjected the trainees to time-honoured hazing rituals. We believed that we could not allow the trainees to be sent out in the world with a chip on their shoulders. It was our solemn duty to knock some sense and humility into them before letting them loose on egotistic clients and creative directors. Both girls and boys would cry in those programmes, thanks to the bullying that went on in the name of hazing.

But for Tanya, everything was water off a duck's back. Whatever criticism was levied at her was subjected to a curious moderation exercise. She would halt in her tracks and listen to the criticism very carefully. When I observed her during such instances I could almost see the wheels turning in her mind.

If she decided that what she'd received was a valid criticism, she would make a change in her behaviour. If she decided it was not constructive, she would dismiss it. For anyone who cared to notice, Tanya's opinion of the criticism received was apparent in her subsequent behaviour.

As I observed her during the training period, I learnt to identify the nuances of her moderation exercise. What she thought was relevant, she imbibed. What she thought was exaggerated or disrespectful, she discarded. But never

ever did she take any negative feedback personally or as a remark on her character. Her work was separate from her personhood and she was careful to maintain that distinction.

Tanya has done extraordinarily well in life. She's jumped fields, changed careers and pivoted with élan. In the last ten years I've not seen many people like her, people who have grown so much or taken on such diverse opportunities. Though we are not in touch any more, I will never forget the girl who was so clear in her thinking and more importantly, her evaluation of herself.

We all are a cocktail of strengths and weaknesses, strong and weak points. We need to learn to see both with an unjaundiced eye. There is absolutely no need to catastrophise weaknesses, whether in ourselves or in the platform we are creating. Life is always about the middle ground. Your platform will never be perfect, but it is also not likely to be tottering on shaky foundations only to collapse like a structure built by a corrupt municipal corporation! And you can always tinker with it later – but launch it at least? Building on strengths and working at minimising weaknesses is a constant endeavour. Even our own prejudices about ourselves should not be allowed to come in the way of marching ahead.

Tanya's level of self-awareness led to her confidence, which allowed her to embrace opportunities with gusto. She didn't let the anxious part of her brain colour her reality and allowed calm reasoning to dictate her behaviour.

I've witnessed what focusing on strengths instead of weaknesses can do to a woman's life. And I've intimately experienced how doing the opposite hurts. The stye is never as large as it seems, and more notably, it is temporary. Regardless of that, you have beautiful eyes. Make the most of them. A little kajal, perhaps?

IN SHORT

- Women tend to minimise their strengths and maximise their weaknesses, in complete contrast to men.
- Constantly worrying about your flaws and making them larger than they are is a sure way to get stuck in a rut.
- If you concentrate on your strengths and work at building on them, it will not only give you the confidence to move forward but also enthuse investors, bosses and colleagues to support you.

Need to Feel Needed

*It's important to set goals which change. Constant endeavour
should be part of our lives.*

—Swami Chinmayananda

It's my experience that women get extremely excited with
the prospect of being needed. Men, meanwhile, stride
through life in the fond belief that they are essential for
the world to exist, so any external validation of this feeling
is really not required. The sun shines on, tides come and
go, and trumpets blow triumphantly only because the male
human walks upon the earth – that's the way they look at
life. Women are not born with this sense of entitlement,
so they struggle to believe they are important and thus
get super excited when someone makes them feel wanted.
(I don't mean that in the Biblical sense as much as the
warm and fuzzy feeling that comes from becoming a core
and beloved part of any ecosystem.)

My first job as a freshly minted management trainee
was at an advertising agency. Those were pre-millennial days
when we were all insecure about our place in the world and
pathetically grateful to the organisations that had deigned
to hire us at a pittance. All of us began our training in the
operations department, which was really just a fancy name
to describe the gofers.

We were the coordinators between the tantrum-throwing, whimsical and crazy gods in the creative department and the beleaguered, stressed-out, work-hard-party-harder servicing types, who were at perpetual war with each other. The creative team was busy sitting on their Olympian heights thinking of the next Cannes-winning headline with which to sell the new detergent. And the servicing team was busy wooing the client at three-hour boozy lunch sessions. It fell on the ops team to do all the drudge work.

Our department's role was that of a plumber, or rather the plumber's assistant. But it was also the department that made things happen. Be it coordinating briefs with writers, writers with designers, layouts with client approval and then back again for changes; running to the typesetter and the printing press to catch the last courier for the release of the ad the next day – we kept the wheels of the organisation in motion.

All of us youngsters enjoyed that role tremendously and felt important and indispensable, especially diffident souls like me. So when that first year was up and we were finally getting transferred to our permanent jobs – strategic planning, client servicing, media planning and the like – I went through a bout of uncertainty and hesitation.

I was doing well, enjoying my work and, most importantly, feeling needed. Why then should I move? The boys in my batch obviously shared none of these doubts. They were raring to get out of their training knickers and the dead-end ops department and march towards the glorious career that indubitably lay ahead of them.

Eventually of course I made the rational and correct decision and joined the rest of my batch in their quest for success. However, it was a salutary lesson on the trap we can fall into if we anchor ourselves around our need to feel needed!

You have all been in situations like this – in organisations or departments where you are respected, liked, successful and (most importantly) vital to their functioning! The CEO thinks you are completely indispensable and your cabin is littered with BEST BOSS IN THE WORLD cups, stickers and wall hangings given to you by an adoring team. Your calendar is filled with meetings and conferences and one-on-ones. You walk into the office and everyone rushes to you, clamouring for your attention. Every moment is action packed and you are the pivot of that action! Atta girl, you say to yourself every morning as you breathlessly rush into work. If any of you have watched *Madam Secretary*, the CBS TV drama series, you'll know that in every episode, when the protagonist walks into office each morning, her team accosts her at the lift with panting tongues and puppy-dog expressions, to apprise her about the latest crisis that has occurred in some part of the world. And off she flies to resolve it, with much aplomb and verve. You are emulating exactly that in your own little niche and heaven seems to have no boundaries at that moment! Only a dunce would want to meddle with anything in that perfect picture!

But is the picture really perfect? Or is being appreciated and not taken for granted such a self-serving luxury for us women that we allow it to stymie our growth?

I don't want to be morbid, but the fact is that women have always lived with the feeling of being unwanted, right from the stage of being undesirable female foetuses to becoming the girl child whose birth is seen as a curse, to being constantly shushed because girls are not supposed to be heard, or rebuked for being too 'noticeable'. It would be infinitely preferable, dear girl, if you did not exist, but since you do, can you be invisible please?

No wonder women are particularly susceptible to this desire to feel needed. The mother who keeps babying her grown-up children, the wife who waits hand and foot on her husband, the secretary who will never share with the temp where she gets that perfect cup of coffee for her boss are all manifestations of this deeply felt need for need!

One of my mentees is the head of a business vertical in a large IT company. She is currently being groomed for a larger role in the organisation. As part of her personal development, I identified a list of milestones that she had to work on at different stages of the mentoring programme. The first six months went past like a dream, with Radha successfully meeting all her deadlines. Then overnight, she froze in her tracks. For the next six months, despite repeated reminders and gently nudging conversations, it seemed to me that she was making no progress at all! I finally had a tough talk with her to figure out what was going wrong. She launched into a detailed explanation of how for the last six months she had been managing her sister's family since said sister had twisted her ankle and needed her help. She was also managing her brother's immigration process to Australia and working with her former boss who had requested her support to finish a couple of projects. And all this while managing an intensive work schedule that required her to be on calls with clients operating in the US, at (obviously) US timings! No wonder she hadn't been able to do anything about her personal growth milestones!

Sheepishly, she admitted that she had a problem with saying no to people who asked her for help. While I admire her Good Samaritan outlook and noble heart, I remain convinced that she was secretly enjoying this ultra-dependence of everyone on her!

Until very recently, I was a manic multitasker, managing home and hearth and travel plans and staff schedules and school projects and laundry services, operating on a schedule any military general would have been proud of! Being praised on an almost daily basis by HD and son for my efficiency (I realised when I grew wiser that they were employing a very convenient motivating strategy with great success), the joy of feeling needed was enough to keep me going like a wildly spinning top. Then one day I realised my misplaced zeal was, err, misplaced. I was burning myself out while also not finding time to do what I truly wanted to do!

So how should we get out of this self-serving and misplaced joy we get in feeling that our tiny worlds would collapse if we were not around to hold them together?

I met Reena when she was a hotshot corporate lawyer in one of the largest legal firms in the country. She was handling an IPR matter for us, which was intricate and long-drawn. Over an extended period of sitting outside the senior counsel's room and amid high court hearings, we got to know each other quite well. She confided in me that while she was enjoying her job, she felt she had started stagnating in her role. As an expert on IP matters, she was much sought after and her views respected within her firm as well as within the legal fraternity. However, she longed to widen her knowledge base beyond her current niche. We won the case and I lost touch with Reena, till I bumped into her at a function where she was receiving an award. In the intervening years, she told me, she had given up her cushy and high-paying job and joined a much smaller firm where she had the opportunity to expand her scope of legal knowledge tremendously.

'I was shit scared to leave my erstwhile firm,' she said. 'I had spent fifteen years there and they gave me tremendous love and respect. My family thought I was demented when I told them I was leaving. I brazened it out at that time, but I was terrified inside.' She grimaced at remembering how tough a decision it had been. But look where she has reached now!

Thanks to our evolutionary and genetic makeup, human beings are wired for security and we find it extremely hard to move out of our comfort zones (and in the case of women, our comforting zones). The fear of the unknown is a powerful motivator to keep us stuck to the status quo. Added to that is the quixotic desire of women to remain ensconced in environments that keep playing 'you are wanted' in an unending feedback loop.

But in the very moments you are feeling the most comfortable and the most needed, you should be asking yourself some uncomfortable questions. Are you learning? Are you growing? Are you adding value to yourself? Or has being mission-critical become more important to you than your personal growth?

When you don't push the boundaries of your potential, you end up wallowing in the soothing but stagnating comfort of a mud bath. This may be relaxing, but it is also debilitating!

Each time you break out of the cocoon you have woven around yourself, you will emerge a stronger and more stunning butterfly, as I witnessed in the case of Reena and many others like her, who were plucky enough to walk out of their secure spaces. And if you are good at your work, you will become mission-critical wherever you are and whatever you do!

To grow, you have to break that cocoon again and again and yet again, however lovingly you may have built it. This cycle will never end. It should not.

IN SHORT

- We all like to belong and enjoy the feeling of being needed, but sometimes it can come in the way of our growth.
- After being at the receiving end of so many challenges and so much negativity from society, a woman is justified in seeking the security of an encouraging workplace and a supportive boss. But it is important to question whether that cocoon is stymieing your growth.
- Have the courage to jump off the cliff. You will be surprised at how strong your wings are and at the gusts of wind sent your way by a benevolent universe, to help you soar higher and higher! Be brave.

Learning to Let Go

*Letting go means to come to the realisation that some people are
a part of your history, but not a part of your destiny.*

—Steve Maraboli

Vinita cornered me at my sister's fiftieth birthday party
recently and launched into a litany about her eighteen-
year career in one of the largest FMCG companies in
the country. She had quit the job suddenly while on an
international posting, and for four years thereafter had been
trying to get back into the same organisation.

It was a social setting so I was listening to her half-
heartedly while enjoying the general bonhomie around me
and the fine whisky. But my ears perked up at her comment
on trying to get back for four years.

'I was one of the fast-trackers in the organisation.
After about fifteen years of consistent A-ratings, I was
sent to work with one of our largest franchisee operations
in Europe,' she recounted. 'I did well there too, increasing
margins by 15 per cent every year. Everyone seemed mighty
pleased with my performance. But then there was an issue
with my boss.'

Here the story got a little muddy. She glossed over the
details of what had actually transpired. 'Suffice to say that
I complained. They offered to shift me to another location.

But I refused,' she told me grimly. 'So I quit and came back to India.'

'Okay, I get it, but then what is this bright idea about trying to get back into the same organisation?' I asked.

'After I came back, I realised I had made a mistake in not accepting their offer to shift me to another operation. I like the organisation very much. I want to go back. I know there are several opportunities for someone like me, with my experience and calibre. But they are not responding,' she replied in a woebegone tone.

'What do you mean you are not getting a response?' I asked.

'Every time I get in touch, they say there is a vacancy. They agree that I am the right fit for it. But then there is radio silence. I have tried across all their verticals, spoken to everyone I know there, but nothing moves,' she said dolefully.

'How long has this been going on?' I enquired, even though I knew the answer by heart now. I wanted to hear it from her again. Most importantly I wanted her to hear what she was saying. 'Four years,' she repeated.

I asked why she hadn't applied anywhere else. 'I want to work only in that organisation. It's the best in its field and I was happy there,' she confessed mournfully.

'My dear Vinita, YOU may want to work there. But THEY obviously don't want you to work for them! Don't you realise that? Otherwise wouldn't you have got something in four years?' I looked at her, exasperated.

'But why?' she wailed. 'I was a star performer!'

I wanted to shake her hard to make her realise the BOP (blindingly obvious point) she was missing! 'Vinita, obviously whatever transpired between you and your erstwhile boss has created some ripples within the organisation that they are not sharing with you.' I enunciated the words kindly but clearly to drive the message home.

'It's so unfair,' she cried. 'I was right and he was wrong.' I sympathised but also pointed out that she was now out of the organisation while he was still there. The hard truth is that organisations tend to believe their current employees rather than former employees. 'But it's so unfair,' she muttered on replay. 'Why don't they tell me the reason?'

I was awash with pity for her but there was not much I could do, so I left her peering into her gin and tonic and softly crooning to the melting ice cubes that life was unjust indeed.

A harsh reality of life is that many times we end up fighting not facts and direct criticisms but spectres of slander and untruths. Phantoms of rumours, backbiting, seniors taking a dislike to us because of their own insecurities and stymieing our growth. But how does one fight something one cannot confront? It's shadow-boxing at best and no one ever won a shadow-boxing contest – not even Muhammad Ali!

One of the reasons we women are not able to rise to the next rung is an unwillingness to step out of our comfort zones in the mistaken belief that being useful, invaluable and irreplaceable is the acme of our career. That attitude constrains growth, as we've already discussed in the previous chapter. The moment you become irreplaceable, you become part of the furniture and fixtures and are likely to get immortalised in the fixed asset register of your organisation rather than get promoted!

The other equally significant reason is that many times women just get stuck in the past. Men on the other hand have an uncanny ability to move on. They are easily able to let go of the good and the bad, the security and the comfort, with an eye firmly fixed on the next role, the higher salary offer or the bigger car.

If you've devoted a sizeable chunk of your life to an organisation, chances are you are invested personally as well. The mistake is when we assume those feelings are mutual. You can be liked, respected and admired, but it is highly unlikely that an organisation or its leadership will be personally invested in you the way you are in them.

Many of us make this mistake repeatedly. We don't get plum assignments, we are left out of the mid-year increment cycle, we don't get the role transfer that we want, all without a single negative word said to us by our bosses. And despite the clear albeit unsaid messaging, we don't get the hint because we weren't told in so many words!

Only on TV and in movies do people get closure from the party who has wronged them. In real life we have to get up, dust off the hurt and move on while learning to cultivate our own moral code.

My friend Priya was extremely attached to the marquee lifestyle brand she was working for. She had literally created the entire brand from scratch after joining a small organisation that had serendipitously innovated its way into being at the forefront of the indigenous handicrafts wave that had hit our fashion industry a decade ago.

She lived, dreamed and breathed the brand and had lovingly worked on its entire DNA, right from the slight curve in its logo to the designing of its hundred stores. But when there was an opportunity to expand it internationally, the role was given to her colleague. Priya took the setback like a trooper, didn't allow it to impact her work and carried on working in her usual cheerful go-getter fashion.

A couple of years later when the company got some serious PE funding, they wanted a COO as part of the succession-planning process. Priya had worked all along with the CEO as his loyal lieutenant, grudging not an iota of the hard work she had put in and the personal life she had sacrificed because of her passion for the brand. But the CEO and rest of the board decided to look outside the firm for candidates.

Priya was devastated. The labour she had put in for over a decade, the late nights, the early-morning flights, the sourcing of artisans by visiting some of the remotest areas of the country in extremely trying travel conditions, the brick-by-brick building of the hundred stores – everything had gone to nought! Life had snatched away from her what she truly deserved, what she had worked hard for with single-minded devotion.

But after a week-long bout of crying herself silly, she got up, hid her puffy eyes behind celebrity-worthy sunglasses, applied blazing red lipstick, went into the office and quit! She encashed her thankfully sizeable stock options and set up an online venture in the same space. Today Priya is the poster child of online platforms and one of the better known and successful names in the e-commerce space.

Can we assume we will always be treated fairly? No. If we are lucky life will deal us only one or two blows. The truly lucky are those who refuse to allow the blows to hinder their progress.

There is a Zen story of two travelling monks who reached a river in the course of their journey. There they met a young woman. Since the river was in full spate, she asked if they could carry her across. One of the monks hesitated, but the other quickly put her on his shoulders, transported her across the water and put her down on the other bank.

She thanked him and departed. The monk who had hesitated remained preoccupied and agitated for quite a long while after that. Finally, unable to hold his silence, he spoke out. 'Brother, our spiritual training teaches us to avoid any contact with women. But you picked that one up on your shoulders and carried her!'

'Brother,' the second monk replied, 'I set her down on the other side while you are still carrying her with you, even now.'

It's an important lesson to remember in life's journey too. The unfair treatment, the needy bosses and the stultifying jobs are best left in the only place they deserve to be – the past. If we have to be swift in our voyages and successful in our ventures, we have no choice but to learn to let go.

IN SHORT

- Life sends many opportunities our way, but it also sends difficulties, challenges, inequities and injustice.
- When we have been treated unfairly, we want to stubbornly fight to correct the wrong done to us.
- Retreating is also a strategy. If we remain stuck in the past the wound will continue to fester and take over a larger part of our lives than it deserves to own.
- It is not necessary that the world will come to our support. We must learn to let go and move on.

Last Woman Standing

Nobody's taller than the last man standing.

—LaMichael James

Let me tell you a story about Manisha, a fiercely ambitious and devil-may-care friend of mine. Manisha studied HR at XLRI, the country's premier human resources institute, around the same time I was earning my MBA stripes at another venerable institution. She proceeded to get a job with a multinational bank straight out of campus and over the next eighteen years, steadily moved up the rung in the finance sector to become VP–HR. During this time, with characteristic aplomb, she had two lovely children, moved cities a couple of times and had a brief stint abroad. She recently returned to the motherland with yet another step up the corporate ladder. She had worked tremendously hard to reach where she is, and when she bought a plush apartment in midtown Mumbai, we all gathered there to toast her success.

Reminiscing about the decades that had flown past too quickly, we compared the bouquets and the battle scars that we had gathered along the way with the comfortable equanimity of distance and middle age. As we nattered away, she reminded me of an incident around five years ago when seething with frustration, she had come over for a venting session. Her immediate boss had quit and they were thinking of replacing him with an outsider. There were various logical reasons being submitted as to why she wasn't being considered for the role. What was evident, but left unsaid, were her two small children. Since the job demanded a fair amount of travel, there were doubts about whether she would be able to cope in this role.

She believed she was capable of taking on the assignment but felt frustrated at the brick walls she kept encountering. Hence the late-night advice seeking and multiple glasses of wine (watered down, since neither of us has a head for alcohol). We plotted and planned what her move should be. Armed with her track record, past accomplishments, a strategy of what she planned to do as GM, a rehearsed answer for addressing the elephant in the room in the form of her ability to manage home and travel, and the advantages she had over an external candidate, she sought an appointment with the head of HR and the CEO. And she walked away triumphantly with the role! We celebrated with un-watered wine and she went on to excel in her new position.

The next few years she remained so busy with the workload the promotion brought her that I rarely got to see her, and then she went abroad.

We talked about her trailblazing career after that one hiccup and admired the rows of trophies she had been awarded, both from her organisation and externally. She proudly told me that she was the only woman from her batch to have become head of HR. As she took me around her new apartment, I saw pictures of the family's international holidays and artefacts collected from trips around the world. Her mother-in-law declared that no woman in their family had attained the heights Manisha had in the workplace, and all of us basked pleasantly in the glow of a job well done. We had all been part of her journey and were so proud of her success. We knew that only 5 per cent of women in India reach the level she had climbed and that gave us a sense of immense satisfaction.

'Now I want to relax,' she smiled. 'I have more than I could ever have wanted.' I looked at her, flummoxed. 'God has been very kind to me and what's the point in slogging on and on? Isn't this enough?' she looked around, inviting me with a flourish to admire the sea view from her flat. Of course I wanted to be supportive; after all she deserved every bit of what she had got. But I was astonished by the change I saw in her.

Where was the fire-eating Manisha who had walked into the CEO's cabin and demanded her boss's job? When had she turned into this self-satisfied and complacent person who was happy to metaphorically hang up her boots? And where had flown her desire to climb more mountains and cross more streams?

Complacency in the workplace is a common fatigue experienced by both men and women. A positive spin all of us put on it is contentment. In some ways, many of us have become successful beyond our wildest dreams. We have markers of prosperity today that we had not even imagined yesterday. The latest BMW, foreign holidays whenever we want, thousands of people working for us, PE funding for our ideas, board directorships. It feels greedy to want more.

After working very hard for most of our careers, there also comes a time where we start feeling that our skills and talents have been utilised to the maximum degree and working for further improvement seems counterintuitive.

We believe we have given unstintingly of ourselves to the world, and now it's payback time, when the world owes us a living.

Both contentment and entitlement, sadly, have an underlying core of self-satisfaction, which I believe is the beginning that spells the end of learning. The mind tends to relax (read, becomes lazy) and that edge that has always been the driver for achievement becomes blunt.

Especially among women, complacency often creeps in when the definition of success becomes the fact that they are the only woman left standing at that level.

A study on women's participation in the Indian workforce, conducted by Anupriya Singh of Lal Bahadur Shastri Institute of Management, revealed that only 5 per cent of working women made it to senior leadership positions in the corporate sector. Women's representation at the board level is currently 2 per cent. Singh found that 48 per cent of women drop out between junior and middle level. At the junior level, women account for 28 per cent of the labour force. It dips to 15 per cent at the middle level, 10 per cent at the senior level and 5 per cent and less thereafter. Thus at senior positions, more often than not, women like Manisha are likely to be the only woman at the table.

No woman sets out to actively compete solely with her women colleagues. But having gone through the wringer over the years, I've witnessed that when you are the only woman left in the room, your source of self-worth suddenly springs from the fact that you are the only woman in the room.

A prevalent trope in media is pitting women against each other. Everywhere you look – movies, TV, books –

women are made to compete with each other, usually for a man's attention. You compete with your sister, never with your brother. You compete with your sister-in-law, never with your brother-in-law. This socialisation further fuels the shift in focus to other women.

Financial security is a privilege that can never be overstated. When we started out with our working lives, it was the driving force behind our efforts. But the importance we place on it later tends to distort our sense of success.

Financial prosperity should not be the marker of our success. It is a happy by-product of it. We can, and should, leverage it to benefit our life as much as possible. But it is toxic to consider it the trophy of our ambition. The world needs our brains, our experience and our creativity. With time and success, it is up to us to define what motivates us when we have achieved comfortable security. From my conversations with women friends – entrepreneurs, lawyers, doctors, bankers, engineers and so on – I've discovered that after financial security, impact creation is the greatest motivator for working people.

The ability to make a difference to people and ecosystems, whether it is our teams or shareholders, is what drives people who've attained success at par with their ambition. I think at every stage of advancement, women need to reassess their motivations for the work they are doing and reimagine the legacy they wish to leave behind.

Why is complacency among senior women a pet peeve of mine? I've observed an interesting conundrum with employees. Among the men who've reached HOD positions and the lone woman among them who's reached the same, I find the latter invariably better than the former. And that's because she's had to work twice as hard and be twice as competent to reach there. She's had to manage so many different roles, pressures and priorities in her life. This makes her a far more evolved and resilient human being.

I feel that by remaining where she is and not aiming higher, she is doing a disservice to both herself and her organisation. Her experience and competence will make her a great leader. But if she's decided that it's not for her, then it's a loss for herself and a loss for the world.

I invite you to reflect deeply about your current state of work and contemplate the questions I asked myself when I felt restless, yet too guilty to explore that dissatisfaction. There is no middle ground in life. Unless we are moving forward, we are sliding backwards. Martin Luther King Jr said it rightly: 'If you can't fly, then run, if you can't run, then walk, if you can't walk, then crawl, but whatever you do, you have to keep moving forward.'

If you are in that lucky 5 per cent of women who have reached almost the top, then you are absolutely justified to take it easy and enjoy the fruits of your labour. No way does my speaking out against complacency imply that your current achievements are not good enough. You must pat yourself on the back. You must feel a very strong sense of entitlement and be extremely proud of yourself. The remaining 95 per cent of your sisters did not make it this far. You are the crème de la crème. You absolutely must celebrate your success.

But after that you must assess your situation. 'This is where I've reached after decades of hard work. These are my talents and skills. Am I happy?' No one else can answer this question for you. Let nobody, including this book, tell you that where you've reached is not good enough. It is only for you to decide whether you've fulfilled your destiny or if you're still in the process of charting it.

If the answer to your self-questioning is that you are where you dreamed you'd be and are happy with it, then kudos to you. But if your self-reflection reveals that this is just one of the goalposts in your journey and not the destination itself, then it is time to get on with it. So proceed, my beauty, and read on.

IN SHORT

- Once we attain a certain position, a modicum of success or an aspired-to lifestyle, we become content with our achievements and settle down.
- But another word for contentment is complacency, which sets in especially when senior women look around the boardroom and see themselves as the lone representative of their sex.
- This sense of self-satisfaction and unwillingness to strive further is one of the several reasons why women reach the CXO level but don't grow beyond it.
- It is heartbreaking to see this, since in most instances a woman CXO is far more competent than the male CXOs around her. This is because she has fought so many more battles to get there.
- If you are genuinely happy with where you've reached and now want to relax, you're perfectly justified in your decision. If not, keep striving and growing. There's more to achieve.

The Lioness and the Dormouse

It's not my job to make you feel like a man.

—Astrid Leong, *Crazy Rich Asians*

Karishma Soni is a fiercely ambitious entrepreneur who turned her doctor father's single laboratory into a three thousand crore global empire. She also happens to be gorgeous and young, two qualities that frequently lead to her getting mistaken for the secretary, while the male junior executive in the room is assumed to be the boss!

Often, even when her identity is not under question, people simply refuse to take her seriously. It's hard for many people to believe that a young and pretty lady is capable of the accomplishments she has to her name. Despite these obstacles, Karishma has built a thriving business empire that continues to grow. And she is not bitter about these undermining experiences.

'While growing up, generations of men have seen women in only two roles – as a mother or a wife. They don't know how to relate to women at the workplace or as equals. They only know that women are either born to take care of men or need men to protect them,' she said in a recent interview.

In an earlier chapter in this book, we discussed how girls in India are trained from childhood to be quiet, to occupy as little space as possible, to not laugh out loud or answer back. For every action there is an equal and opposite reaction. So it is that our boys are rewarded for being boisterous. But this unequal parenting goes far beyond permitting boys to roll about in the mud and laugh with abandon or not policing their clothes, companions and life choices.

When little boys are constantly raised at the expense of little girls, they continue to expect the same behaviour throughout their lives. Men grow up to see themselves as the centre of the universe and all the women in their lives as assorted satellites fated to orbit around their glorious sun! This is a great disservice not only to women but also to men. We teach them to derive their sense of identity and fulfilment from their roles as protectors and providers and when that role comes into question, it results in a shattering sense of insecurity. Another consequence of this upbringing is the male ego, an all-consuming, all-pervasive beast that requires constant fodder and nourishment.

HD's aunt is a renowned eye surgeon. Sheila Aunty is a feisty woman and continues to do multiple and complicated eye surgeries even at the age of seventy-two. She is confident, bold and indefatigable when it comes to her iconic eye centre. At work she knows exactly what she is doing and dispenses eye care and advice with a surefootedness that is born out of finely honed talent and the experience of a forty-two-year career. The other day we visited her residence to meet the extended family who had gathered there for Diwali, and I was completely mystified by Sheila Aunty's wifely avatar at home! She was meek, docile and tentative in front of Raj Uncle, her husband, who is a retired college principal and seemed to be running his house in exactly the same manner that he ran his college! He ordered her around peremptorily, was dismissive when someone complimented her on an award she had won and quite churlish in his behaviour with her.

'Sheels is so poor at managing the house,' he told us peevishly, when there was a slight delay in the food being served. And Aunty had just come back from her clinic, whilst Uncle Pompous had been sitting on his backside reading the paper the entire morning! We all jumped to her rescue as she flapped around helplessly trying to set the table, while apologising profusely to him and all of us!

I was so angry that I was a hair's breadth away from kicking him! It still maddens me when I think about that incident, so much so that I am actually punching furiously at the keyboard as I write this down! I was angry not only with him but also with Sheila Aunty for putting up with his boorishness. She had been our heroine and role model when we were growing up, and to see her behave like a wimp was a huge let down that day.

Examples of 'the male as centre-piece' are littered throughout Indian literature, cinema and TV. From *Devdas* to everyday *saas-bahu* serials, women bend backwards, forwards and contort themselves in every angle possible to appease the troubled and brooding hero. His needs come first, his feelings are paramount and woe betide the world if the rotis served to him are not freshly made and piping hot!

But perhaps the instant example that comes to mind is the Jaya Bhaduri, Amitabh Bachhan starrer *Abhimaan*. The 1973 film by Hrishikesh Mukherjee sees popular singer Subir (Bachhan) entranced by the soulful, melodic voice of village girl Uma (Bhaduri). He falls in love with her and they get married. Subir convinces Uma to enter showbiz. But when her popularity outshines his own, cracks appear in the marriage.

Even though Uma harbours no desire for fame and is ready to give up singing professionally, it's too late. The couple is driven apart by Subir's jealousy. This being a Bollywood film of course, things work out eventually and they reconcile after some twists and turns – most significantly Subir confronting his own unfair rage and behaviour.

In real life things rarely work out this well, as the couple, on whose life *Abhimaan* was based, would tell you. Roshanara Khan became Annapurna Devi to marry Pandit Ravi Shankar, a disciple of her father Alauddin Khan. But the marriage became strained soon after as Ravi Shankar became jealous of the rave reviews his wife's public performances earned.

In a new biography titled *An Unheard Melody: Annapurna Devi, An Authorised Biography*, writer Swapan Kumar Bandopadhyay describes how bitter Shankar became when his wife's music performances outshone his own:

'She was on the rise. The connoisseurs hailed her as great. The surbahar also helped to establish her supremacy, because it is a more difficult instrument than the sitar, heavier and more satisfying musically. Ravi was justifiably jealous. And so he elicited a vow from his wife that she would no longer play in public,' writes Bandopadhyay.

Annapurna kept her vow. She never played publicly again, even though she and Shankar separated soon after. She kept a select roster of students and passed her craft to them. But while Shankar rose to become a music legend worldwide, Annapurna Devi's art was lost to the world forever.

These may be dramatic and extreme examples rather than the rule, but the fact still remains that working women even today believe that if their success is likely to lead to discord at home, it is better to take a backseat. Despite their accomplishments, they immediately resort to the childhood training of erasing themselves to accommodate their spouses' misguided sense of entitlement.

Recently at a panel discussion on women empowerment in the workplace, a speaker narrated an anecdote about his company. They wanted to promote a woman to a senior position – a position the bosses felt she richly deserved. He brought her in to discuss the move. But instead of happy cheer, her disposition showed tremendous unease and discomfort. She flatly refused the promotion. The manager was stunned and insisted on knowing why she would not accept the role. It took much cajoling before she finally revealed what was going on in her head. She said she could not accept the promotion since her salary would then become higher than her husband's!

I was slack-jawed for a while upon hearing this. But now I realise actions like this are more commonplace than we realise. We don't hear about it because we don't talk about it.

Over the years some conversations about women and inequality in the workplace – sexual harassment, equal pay, double standards, etc. – have gained volume. There are some topics we actively discuss and practices we move to ban. But stories like this rarely get revealed because the women making these adjustments feel guilty and hypocritical even as they martyr themselves for peace at home.

The quick switch that Sheila Aunty routinely practised of playing the doormat at home after being the boss at work, the handing over of all financial decisions to men, the ease with which women become supportive listeners and cheerleaders of their men's exploits, the hiding of the award won at work lest it upset the big guy at home are all symptomatic of this malaise.

However, increasingly I see that the next generation of women is not willing to play second fiddle at home. They are staunchly refusing to be quieter, plainer and more colourless versions of themselves in social or domestic environments.

When after twenty-five years of being married I apologetically requested a separate bathroom for myself, my young and recently married niece was flabbergasted. 'But Apu Aunty, that was my first condition for getting married,' she squealed. 'We also have a marriage manifesto,' she solemnly informed me. 'What does it contain?' I asked her, puzzled. 'Either of us can stay separately if our work requires it. We will take one independent holiday each with our friends. Both of us will take equal time off when we have a baby,' she rattled off at express speed. 'And most certainly, no uncle jokes!' she grinned naughtily. 'What's that?' I wondered. 'He will not ever crack pathetic uncle jokes like "Heh, heh, see how well she has trained me," if someone sees him doing household chores!' she said, pointing an admonishing finger at her beaming husband.

My heart blossomed with pride while listening to her. I was supremely impressed and thrilled with her confidence and her husband's genial demeanour. Our sons are growing up with a healthy sense of self; they are comfortable in their skins. And our daughters are growing up with unapologetic ambition and derring-do. They are making sure that both sexes walk tall and stand shoulder to shoulder with each other. Our girls are refusing to tiptoe around the male ego and equally our boys are sweeping their partners in their arms, and twirling merrily all over the ashes of the bonfires of vanity!

We must have done something right in their upbringing. Who knows? Maybe it's finally time that the child truly became the father of the man and we get reverse mentored by our daughters who can teach us a thing or two. Maybe that dawn has indeed come when we learn to be true to ourselves, not by hiding but by showcasing our coloured plumes in all their vibrant glory in each and every moment we live.

IN SHORT

- While working women have been fighting a long and arduous battle in the world outside, they have also had to contend with the male ego at home.
- To keep home affairs calm and male feathers unruffled, many times they choose to mute their achievements and accept secondary-citizen status at home.
- But millennials are far more confident than earlier generations. The millennial girl wants to be acknowledged publicly and privately for her triumphs and accomplishments.
- Maybe we should be reverse mentored by this generation and own our successes on every occasion.

Subconscious Bias

Stereotypes fall in the face of humanity. We human beings are best understood one at a time.

—Anna Quindlen

On a visit to a well-known tech firm to conduct a workshop with their women employees, I was most impressed with the large pool of competent and talented women in their middle management. But I was sorely disappointed that there was not even a single woman employee in the senior leadership team.

When I quizzed Anand, the CEO, he was mournful about this. He assured me most solemnly that he was a pro-woman recruiter, desperately wanted gender diversity in his office but couldn't find any women in his team who were ready or keen to take on the stressful responsibilities that a senior role entailed. He informed me that he personally had been headhunting extensively for a couple of critical positions but had been unable to find any women to fit those roles, either inside or outside his organisation.

I was very pleased with his enthusiasm and earnestness in correcting this unfair imbalance, left him looking glumly at more CVs and went away, delighted with having met a male leader who was such an ardent advocate of diversity.

But a completely different tale met me while talking to the women in the organisation during the workshop. I started the session by asking them what was holding them back from accepting promotions for the next level. Did they believe they didn't have the necessary qualifications or did they believe they would be unable to cope with the pressures of senior managerial roles? I wanted to understand why they were voluntarily choosing to stagnate instead of moving ahead.

Their collective protestations stunned me. They told me they were dying to be given more responsibilities and indeed were thirsty for opportunities to prove themselves, but were not being offered those roles. When I asked the HR team present at the workshop why they hadn't pushed for filling those vacant senior positions with women from their existing talent pool, pat came the reply that all the senior roles involved late nights, heavy travel, unreasonable client expectations and a huge amount of pressure. They believed that their women employees would not be able to cope with these insane demands and would refuse to take these assignments or would end up burning out or compromising on their work or family if they did agree! As good employers, they didn't want to impose such a burden on the women.

But before making these assumptions, had anyone actually checked with these ladies whom they were so valiantly protecting, and asked what their opinion on the matter was? There was deafening silence in the room when I asked this question.

Each time someone has asked me if I've encountered any bias in the workplace because of being a woman, I have always said no. I have always believed that in my career I have got the same opportunities as any man in my position. But this experience brought those assumptions to a screeching halt. I started looking back and wondering about all the opportunities that had possibly passed me by because nobody even cared to check whether I was ready for them, in the false assumption that I wasn't. How would I even know that I was the subject of bias if I didn't even know it was happening to me?

Patriarchy has long been the popular villain for gender inequality at the workplace and elsewhere. Men have been in hierarchical positions of power from the beginning of existence. Thus ingrained in them and in the systems around them is a view that women are inferior, less capable and in constant need of protection and support. In its most benign state, this inculcates a systemic response geared towards making women weaker than they are, than they need to be or deserve to be.

Anand's bias, despite his pro-women stance, was not hypocritical. He had been indoctrinated with a stereotype that was not true about the women in his team and he didn't even realise that this bias existed in his mind. He was certainly well-intentioned when he worried that he would put extraordinary pressure on his women managers by promoting them, but he also was being unfair to his women managers by being paternalistic.

I assess Anand's bias not from a moral high ground, but with the inside knowledge only the guilty can possess. I once hired a CEO, Hitesh, for one of the companies I manage after doing due diligence on his background. He had the right credentials and his references were stellar. Added to that he gave all of us a feeling of great comfort and confidence with his deep gruff voice, measured tone and solid demeanour (he was well over six feet tall and built like a barrel). All of us felt assured that he could navigate the company through any storm. He spent two years at the organisation and then one day quit abruptly, citing unexplained personal reasons.

His sudden departure got me, the HR team and the people who worked directly with him searching within ourselves for the reasons for his move. After a lengthy analysis we realised that he had been unable to handle the pressure of the three months prior to his resignation. The organisation had been facing headwinds and revenue pressures at that time. I was puzzled that he threw in the towel when the going got tough because innate strength was a quality I'd always associated with him.

Only once I started connecting the dots and reviewing his performance, not only in our company but also in previous organisations, did the mystery begin to resolve itself. Closer inspection revealed that whenever a significant crisis had arisen in the organisations under his charge, he had not been the one to resolve it. He had preferred to ignore the problem rather than taking charge and facing it head-on.

Hitesh's physical attributes matched accurately the stereotype of the strong and silent alpha male who comes striding out of the sunset to solve the community's woes with the music score of a spaghetti western movie playing in the background. His statuesque demeanour and deep bass voice communicated leonine strength and dependability to me, while inside he was just a little mouse! I grudgingly admitted to myself that I, like Anand, had acted on bias rather than on empirical evidence.

At any given time, the human brain is bombarded with eleven million pieces of information. We can only handle forty. To navigate the world without being inundated and overwhelmed, the brain creates patterns that help sort this information. Forming stereotypes is one such pattern. And by assuming that people behave according to a certain stereotype, we begin acting out of bias. We are also genetically coded to be positively biased towards people similar to us.

Once we take into consideration that the majority of managers and recruiters are men, the absence of women in the upper echelons of corporate India begins to make a lot of sense. People will naturally choose candidates they identify with the most.

Even the most well-meaning of us, both men and women, are biased. Instead of railing against a genetic trait that skews the scales against women, let's ask what we can do to help people around us (including ourselves) step out of the narrow corridors of perception bias.

The incentive to dismantle subconscious bias lies not just in diverse gender-equal hiring. When leaders take the time to assess their preconceived notions, they enhance their level of objective comprehension and critical reasoning skills. In short, they become better at their jobs.

As far as gender bias goes, there is unfortunately no quick fix for reaching into the subterranean regions of male minds and shaking out the cobwebs. The only way to deal with these perceptions is to co-opt more and more men into the diversity conversation. Every time I speak on this issue at any organisation, I ask that men also be part of the proceedings. There are several initiatives across the globe where men are increasingly being encouraged to be part of this process of recognising and thus changing subconscious behaviours and mindsets, and we must all actively support such initiatives.

Equally we need to be patient not in accepting but in explaining to men what we believe qualifies as biases. The famous 'silent treatment' women adopt to manage conflict will not work here! It is imperative to call out the big as well as the small biases we see playing out around us every day. Don't call me 'sweetheart', don't assume it's the male at the table who will pay the bill, don't automatically decide that my drink will be a mocktail and look shocked when I ask for a strong shot, and yes HD cooks and I don't! The more time women spend discussing with men what they want, what they value and what they don't, the more we will be able to remove the misconceptions in their minds. Equally we will understand their point of view. Which is yet another reason we need more women at the workplace, in the boardrooms and at the negotiating tables.

Finally, we have to consciously stop ourselves from playing to a stereotype. The Pet, the Mother, the Seductress are some of the slots we naturally and effortlessly manoeuvre ourselves into, like obedient clockwork dolls in a dystopian fairy tale. And every time a woman leaves her job to stay at home, it reinforces the perception that the workplace is not her natural domain and God always intended womenfolk to be housewifely.

Biases are created out of patterns we reinforce repeatedly. Mindfully and laboriously, we need to erase these behaviours in ourselves and in doing so, erase them from the minds of all the folk around us.

IN SHORT

- The human brain perpetuates stereotypes because that is the only way it can make sense of complex information and the data overload it is bombarded with.
- Thus despite best efforts, the stereotypes operating around women continue to be part of the subconscious biases that exist at the workplace.
- Women get slotted in traditional moulds unconsciously and because the biases are subterranean, they become very difficult to challenge.
- The only way to erase these biases is to call them out constantly.

All the Single Ladies

I got my own back.

—Maya Angelou

The prejudices and biases we discussed in the previous chapter have become such an inescapable part of the world surrounding women that we don't even notice them any longer. People assume that women can't drive well or open a can or change the light bulb and mostly we give these biases a pass and let them think whatever they want. Partly because we are fed up of proving a point all the time and partly because it is quite convenient to get someone more manly to open the can or drive us where we want to go. Much like my son pretending that there was a Santa Claus way beyond the regulation age of awakening to myths till we started wondering whether he was a bit dim. Only to realise that by age two he had quite adeptly grasped the reality, but chose to keep up the pretence in order to get his presents!

Beyond a point I don't get agitated if at a party you ask my husband where he works and what he does and then condescendingly ask me about my favourite city for shopping! I smile beatifically, pat the sofa next to me and say, 'Come sit by my side and I will tell you all about Marrakesh's hidden markets and Le Marais in Paris.'

But the preconceptions that surround bachelor girls make even a hardened pragmatist such as me gasp. Having got married in my early twenties, I completely bypassed the peculiar barbs that single women in India are bombarded with, but some of the stories they tell me would try the patience of any monk.

For example, I recently met a fabulous young lady at a talk I gave at an SME forum. She's a successful entrepreneur in her own right who's done a brilliant job in turning around and scaling up the business she inherited from her late father. Her life story intrigued me so much that we chatted for hours.

Ayesha is single. I was fascinated not by her singledom but the story of how it has affected her work life. She told me of a recent audit review at her firm. As is the norm, every audit review ends with a risk-management discussion with the senior management. Post the review, the auditor asked her what she viewed as the biggest risk to her business. 'Me,' she told him nonchalantly.

I almost choked on my coffee as she recounted this to me. Did she really think she was the biggest risk to her business? 'Well, of course I don't think that,' she clarified. 'But this issue has cropped up on various occasions in my life. So I decided in the spirit of full disclosure to be forthcoming with the auditor about the challenges facing the organisation and tell him what so many people have repeatedly told me,' she smiled naughtily.

Take for example an encounter she had in her early days as boss of the company. Ayesha's father had recently passed away. She had unexpectedly become the face of the business at a very young age but was eager to shake things up and accelerate growth. She was twenty-seven at the time. She'd gone to meet a big industrialist to pitch some ideas. The industrialist asked her, 'Why should I give my business to you?' She was ready with what made her company the best suited for the job and rattled off all the reasons with great verve and enthusiasm. While agreeing with all her claims, the industrialist shot back, 'Yes, all this is fine, but I have one fundamental issue with your business.'

'What?' she asked, slightly fazed.

'I see you as the biggest risk to your business. Tomorrow if you get married and move away, what will happen to your company and by association my supply?' he queried.

She smiled as she recounted this story. 'It's been ten years. I am thirty-seven now and the people I meet still consider me the biggest risk to the business. The foremost question on the minds of prospective investors and collaborators is the risk of being left in the lurch when I'm suddenly swept off my feet by a prince charming and leave everything I've worked so hard for years to build – both mine and my father's legacy – to ride off into the sunset with him.'

The question seemed completely absurd to her. Why would she leave everything and go away? But apparently that's how men see single women's work – as placeholders while they wait for their prospective husbands and even more prospective offspring. Getting married sometime in the future was a vague possibility in Ayesha's case, but what was crystal clear to anyone who knew her was the dedication and hard work she had put into reviving her dad's business and turning it around so dramatically. But regrettably the subtext after every such meeting was that her ability to work would be forever and irrevocably altered once she got married. While it was gratifying that Ayesha was handling these prejudices with a sense of humour, the fact that this question would not have even been contemplated had Ayesha been an Ayush was galling in the extreme.

As the only single woman in a firm with an otherwise decent representation of female employees, Indrani explains to me how her marital status disadvantages her. Her boss always asks her to stay back and finish the work of other women. 'Let her go home. She has small children waiting for her. You finish the work. After all, you have no such responsibilities,' is his reasoning.

Often, bosses refuse to entertain pay raise requests from single women: 'Why do you need a pay raise? You don't have a family to provide for.' It frustrates these women very much. 'What do you mean? So what if I am single? Won't I have financial requirements of my own? Don't I have parents to look after or a future to secure?' they rant to me. Married people, or even unmarried men, are never asked to justify their raises. An unmarried woman has to justify even her paycheck.

Mehnaz is the thirty-five-year-old COO of a small financial services firm. She has been constantly hearing barbs over her unmarried state since her mid-twenties, under the guise of well-meaning advice.

'It's not that I am against marriage,' she wailed to me. 'But I can't get hitched to just anybody for the sake of getting married. He has to be the right guy.'

Unfortunately, she has rarely ended up meeting the 'right' man who is not intimidated by her independence!

She finally got so fed up of the pressure that she agreed to meet a few men. 'From the beginning I knew it was doomed,' she told me about her interaction with one of them. She was in Goregaon and the guy was in Worli, but he expected her to meet him there. 'He wasn't even willing to meet me halfway. I had to go all across Mumbai to where he was, because after all HE was the superior partner in the future relationship.'

Nonetheless she swallowed her misgivings and braved the Mumbai traffic to conduct her personalised swayamvar. The first question posed by the shortlisted groom was, 'So do you intend to work after marriage?' 'I am the COO of an organisation. Obviously, I intend to work after marriage,' she retorted incredulously. 'Maybe you can consider becoming a teacher if you insist on working,' he magnanimously suggested. 'Why teacher?' she asked.

'Not that I have anything against teachers but I was so flummoxed with that suggestion that I just had to know,' she recalls.

'If you are a teacher, then you can be at home after half day to take care of our children,' said the husband and dad-in-waiting coyly! Suffice to say Mehnaz is clinging to her singledom fiercely after her brief dip into the dating pool.

Gloria Steinem aptly said, 'We are becoming the men we wanted to marry.' Today's educated working woman does not need to marry for security, but she certainly wants an equal partner in every sense of the term. Most of my single women friends are not single by choice; they would like to have a spouse to share life's ups and downs with. But they rarely encounter a male who is comfortable with the concept of marital equality. And in the absence of suitable choices, they would much rather remain single than settle for someone who would diminish them.

Though she rarely sets out to make a statement, some view the single woman as a radical. She doesn't exist for her husband or children. She exists for herself. Her salary is not to pay for school tuitions or family vacations but to spend on herself. She is such a threat to a well-ordered patriarchal world that she needs to be controlled and censored at every turn and punished for her choices. Let her stay back late, give her extra work, don't pay her much money – these are the punishments for the husband and children-less nature of her life.

Others may not see her as a threat, but she is a lesser being to them. She exists to make life easier for married folks who have too much pressure at home and outside it. If unmarried women can take that pressure off, well that's because they should. What else are they going to do with all the extra time and money they have?

'If I am single, I must be promiscuous,' my friend Shirleen says of how the world views her. 'At the very least I should have no hang-ups about sleeping with anyone in the office kind enough to take note of my attractiveness.'

Shirleen recounts an incident – rather, a horror story – from when she had just started working. She was young, inexperienced and easy pickings in the eyes of a predatory boss. He showered her with inappropriate remarks and sexually laden innuendos at work. Initially she shrugged those off with an uneasy laugh because she didn't have the courage to stand up to him.

One weekend he started texting her, sending compliments about her looks and asking her out for a drink. She didn't know how to refuse politely, so she didn't reply at all. On Monday morning her boss icily commented in front of the whole team that Shirleen obviously wasn't a dependable person since she didn't even bother to see her messages over the weekend.

After fortifying herself with self-talk, Shirleen went into his cabin to 'explain' herself. She told her boss that her strict conservative father commandeered her phone during weekends to curb any 'disreputable' activity. The boss was embarrassed to know her father may have read his flirty texts and left her alone for the rest of the time she worked there.

For Shirleen this was a bitter victory. She had protected herself by infantilising herself. The fact that she was an independent adult was of no consequence to her boss. Her consent, or lack thereof, had not been a barrier to his advances. But he respected the fact that she was her father's property, a fiction she had sold to him by undermining herself.

Every time I hear examples of the myriad, nuanced and delicate ways in which my supremely strong single friends navigate a muddled and unfair world, I am filled with awe and respect. In the face of a society determined to define their unworthiness, they are fiercely and unashamedly living life on their own terms. And having boatloads of fun while doing so.

One of my single friends has chucked up her career and has become a healer full time. She told me, 'I have saved up enough to be financially secure and I don't have anyone to leave my money to. So why shouldn't I do exactly as I please?' The last I heard is that she is off to Glastonbury, which apparently is the heart chakra of the world (!), to conduct a healing workshop! Now isn't that cool! A freelance writer friend took off to Himachal on a whim to live in a village and volunteer at the local school. Looking at the breathtakingly beautiful updates of her bohemian lifestyle on Facebook, I realised that once upon a time matrimony may have been the final prize to aspire to. But no longer is it true.

Now more than ever, the world has become boundary-less and label-less and in becoming so, it has become truly empowering. Today there are many different and differing ways to live, each offering its own rewards and heartbreaks. And if my bachelorette friends' adventures are anything to go by, the joys of singledom are spectacular in their own right.

IN SHORT

- Single women have been the frontrunners in demonstrating to the world that women and men are equal and deserve to be treated on par.
- By flying in the face of traditional expectations and conservative mindsets, they have indicated their freedom and demonstrated their courage.
- As we see the numbers of single women increasing in a more open and diverse world, we need to stand in support with them so that they have the space and the empowerment to live life on their own terms.

Token Woman

Definitions belong to the definer, not the defined.

—Toni Morrison

I had imagined I would feel a great many things when I finally got to sit on a board – the relish of having made it; the satisfaction of being surrounded by top achievers across different fields; the reflected glory of the polish from all that chrome, glass and leather around me. I was savouring the thought of saying, 'With great power comes great responsibility,' with a bravely suffering look to people all around me. What I had not imagined even in my wildest of fancies was that I would be deified – albeit in the 'Goddess who must be revered but largely ignored' fashion!

It took some time to dawn on me what it meant to be the lone woman in a boardroom populated largely by alpha males who at first glance looked like grizzled versions of extras from *Men in Black*. There were flowers, compliments and plenty of references such as, 'For heaven's sake, there's a lady present!' Self-appointed knights dressed in, err, black, regularly rushed to open and close doors for me. I was gallantly told by all the gentlemen in the room how I had enlivened the previously dull proceedings with my fair presence. One respectable member of the board coyly divulged to me that I had brought much-needed glamour into the boardroom. Universally all my ideas were commented upon and exclaimed over with much ado, and equally universally politely dismissed. And that was if I ever got a chance to complete my sentences or be heard in the first place!

Getting talked over is a familiar foe for all women, but the glamour comment got my goat. 'They think I'm here to be glamorous, do they?' I seethed to myself. To countermand this completely ridiculous perception I immediately twirled my wand around and became the absolute opposite of the glamour queen – the earth mother!

Now the self-appointed matron in the boardroom, I cajoled, scolded and disciplined my way through most meetings. I would sternly offer admonishment or kindly mete out criticism to men two decades senior to me. I dictated agendas as though I were setting homework and offered the solace of my cosy shoulders to the management team after tough meetings. I remember an instance when I actually came within a whisker of patting the CEO on his shoulder and saying 'there, there' after a particularly brutal quarter results meeting. He was looking at me longingly for exactly that reason, but I desisted (I think)!

There couldn't have been a better mother than me and we soon settled into a happy family routine at the board meetings thereafter.

Many senior women I know ask my advice on what it takes to get onto a board. They believe that getting onto a board is mandatory to reach the next rung in their careers since it showcases their achievements to people outside their organisation and prepares them for larger responsibilities. While this is certainly true, I do urge them to reflect on a few things.

Firstly, I tell them it is important to judge what their contribution will be on the board. Will they bring a specific functional perspective or a particular industry expertise that is missing? What outside angle can they bring that will synchronise with what the board requires? It is critical not to get onto a board just to be a mute spectator.

Secondly, being on a board is no longer a simple matter. With the Companies Act, 2013 becoming more and more draconian with time, there are a lot more expectations from board members in terms of monitoring the governance practices of an organisation and being mindful that the business is being run with integrity and diligence. By sitting on a board and attending four to six meetings a year, one will never learn what's happening inside the company. Despite the many questions one may ask or how engaged one is, no one will ever get to know the intricacies of the organisation from the distance of a board chair. And thus it has now become more of a liability than an asset to be on a board.

The third and most important thing I tell my women friends is to truly understand the issues that come with being the solitary woman director in the room.

Alas, being the token woman on the board comes with a mountain load of baggage that needs to be dealt with delicately and firmly. Most organisations treat women directors as a tedious requirement that the law expects them to comply with. The male board members treat women as if they are a different species altogether and very much an inferior sort at that.

Finally, women themselves subconsciously behave in yet another fashion, by either assimilating or resisting these treatments. Both these behaviours unfortunately lead to the same tapered end of becoming typecast, as it happened to me in my starring role as mother of the board.

In 1983, Harvard business professor Rosabeth Moss Kanter identified four distinct role traps that women habitually get pigeon-holed into while trying to navigate male bastions of power. These stereotypes arise mainly from men's perception of a woman in charge in the workplace. But more importantly, they also endure because of women's willingness to conform to these roles.

The most common stereotype of the woman at work is the Seductress. A woman who takes pride in her grooming and likes to dress well is immediately labelled a distraction in the workplace. Her efforts at climbing the corporate ladder are looked on with suspicion. People readily believe that she schmoozed her way to the top rather than acknowledge she may be talented and hardworking enough to have earned the role. The Seductress's femininity is what places distrust upon her. Both men and women are wary of her and that's why when my fellow board member told me that I had enhanced the glamour quotient in the room, I pivoted immediately towards the polar opposite maternal mode.

The Mother is a typical and the most traditional role a woman in the workplace embodies. She is completely non-threatening sexually and will be described as a frump, matron or schoolmarm in terms of appearance. She is caring, compassionate and warm. Her leadership is valued in the emotional labour she provides and not in the industry expertise she brings to the table.

The third stereotype Kanter talks about is the sweet, cute and girly mascot of womanhood, which is adopted by the contingent for amusement – the Pet. She is teased and mocked relentlessly. She will put up with the teasing lest people think she is not a good sport. The childish silliness assigned to the Pet undermines her credibility. This cutie pie bimbette is much loved for her antics. But she will never be taken seriously. She won't be considered for promotions and important leadership positions. She is even going to be excluded from serious conversations and decisions about the organisation.

The fourth stereotype is the assertive and no-nonsense woman at work, the Iron Maiden. Unlike the Seductress it is her competence and not her sexuality that makes her a threat. She is described as tough, mean, hard, scary and mannish. The Iron Maiden is a bully who lives for her work, has no personal life and no feminine allures to soften her harsh edges.

If she were a man, the Iron Maiden would be described as a go-getter, a deal-closer and a leader. But because she is a woman, she is bossy. Think Margaret Thatcher or our own Indira Gandhi. Modern time has seen labels like feminazi and man-hater added to the traditional canon of descriptors reserved for such a stereotype. The Iron Maiden can, and likely will, make it to the top. But she will be considered horrid for doing so.

Why do women bother substantiating the silly stereotypes they get endowed with? For Kanter, who has done ground-breaking research work on tokenism throughout her career, the answer is simple. It is easy and sometimes a matter of survival to concede to a dominant culture because it can be the path of least resistance to success.

Bitch or Bimbette. Mother or Seductress. Either we willingly walk into a box presented to us. Or we resist walking into one box by walking into another ourselves. We forget that the choice to not squeeze ourselves into a set precedent is ours and ours alone. Are we aware that each time we choose to embody a particular stereotype, we are complicit in accepting the treatment we get?

So what can we do? Across the world, women are fighting back. For example, the late Aston University professor Judith Baxter re-analysed Kanter's four role traps in the modern context and was pleasantly surprised by what she found. Not only did she see newer, more positive versions of these archetypes that women have coined for themselves to resist traditional power structures in the workplace, like Queen Bee, Superwoman and Xena (the warrior princess), but she also saw women leaders in the workplace skilfully navigating between the four roles to fulfil their professional objectives.

Baxter highlighted the example of Germany's chancellor, Angela Merkel, who flits between iron-fisted chancellor or 'mother' at home and 'charming female bantering with male heads of state' at Eurozone tête-à-têtes. This reclamation of agency from labels that have been thrust upon us to more proactive styles that we mindfully choose to adopt is indeed cause for celebration and a worthy example for all of us to follow.

In any case, owning multifaceted leadership styles is the natural next step ahead not only for women but also for men, as we learn to work in a volatile and ambiguous environment requiring flexible managerial skills.

The typical binary world is increasingly losing its context, especially as we deal with a generation of millennials and Gen Z, unencumbered as they are both by historical hangovers and conventional mindsets.

So as you move in to claim your role as a leader in an amorphous new age, can you be Earth Mother in Season One and morph seamlessly into Seductress in Season Two and then jump to Iron Maiden in the Finale? Can you?

IN SHORT

- Traditional stereotypes surrounding women have typically fallen into four distinct roles traps – the Seductress, the Pet, the Iron Maiden and the Mother.
- Unfortunately, women have chosen the path of least resistance and played to these roles in order to fit social norms and the dominant patriarchal culture.
- We need to break out of these set patterns of behaviour in order to shatter these stereotypes forever.
- By creating newer and more multi-faceted leadership styles we will evolve a more relevant managerial style to deal with the changing contexts of a new-age workforce and work environment.

Finding Sisterhood

Sisters in battle, I am shield and blade to you. As I breathe, your enemies will know no sanctuary. While I live, your cause is mine.

—Leigh Bardugo, *Wonder Woman: Warbringer*

I was delighted when my long-time friend Gauri finally agreed to have lunch with me. We used to be thick as thieves and our monthly lunch meetings had been both witness and markers of our progress, from the twenty-five rupees per plate meals at Mahesh Lunch Home (one small fried fish each and one plate of rice with free curry) to the five-star meals at some of the hallowed restaurants of the Taj. But then she became a partner at one of the top management consultancy firms in the country and scheduling a get-together with her became well-nigh impossible.

It's no secret that the work environment at management consultancy firms is ruthlessly competitive and making one's way to the top is a long and difficult journey – one that Gauri had been assiduously working her way through. She had finally succeeded and was now one of the only two female partners among a hundred male partners.

But while the scent of victory was sweetly perfumed, it was also accompanied by sharp and unpleasant gusts of performance pressure and stress. Every day Gauri left home at 7.30 in the morning, returning well after 9 p.m. I knew the last time she had taken a vacation was five years ago so I was lucky that she had been able to sneak away for lunch.

When Gauri walked in for our date, I was stunned to see how haggard she looked. I had expected her to be tired and overworked, but certainly not so desolate. Overruling her plea that she was on a diet, I ordered her favourite dishes and once she had polished off her beloved tiramisu, I gave her my signature basilisk look and launched into my interrogation.

'So what's up? Spill the beans without leaving out a single beanlet. And don't waste your breath telling me all is well. It clearly is not.'

One of the biggest advantages of a decades' long relationship is that no one wastes time posturing, so the beans did gush out forthright!

I knew about the internal politics and external demands of Gauri's job and she informed me that she was dealing quite adroitly with those. Managing difficult clients, ensuring expected billings, surpassing targets and the horrendous travel schedule, all the expectations from a partner were grist to her mill. She said that she was thriving in such a hardcore environment. So, no. It wasn't the work pressure that was getting to her. It was the fact that she had no one to talk to!

The only other woman partner at her firm was posted in another city. Most days, and most meetings, she was the only woman in the room. She was good friends with all her colleagues, but she had no way of letting off steam and was rarely able to let her hair down at work the way she saw the men around her doing, notwithstanding their thinning pates.

'I am lonely,' she confessed morosely.

I wanted to hug her tightly, hoping that the warmth of a friend's non-judgemental embrace would give her some succour. Like Munnabhai, I am a big believer in the *'jaadu ki jhappi'* concept, but try as we did to prolong the lunch and the brief magic of soul-sisterly warmth we had created around ourselves, it was soon over. We both returned to our offices, each to fight her own war.

Sociologists Tetyana Pudrovska and Amelia Karraker studied thirteen hundred middle-aged men and fifteen hundred middle-aged women for a paper titled 'Gender, Job Authority and Depression'. They found that job authority increases symptoms of depression in women but decreases them in men. These results are not surprising. The social isolation faced by women in authority leads them to suffer from a poorer state of mental health than women at lower rungs. According to the researchers, women in senior positions had to also deal with a barrage of interpersonal tensions, negative stereotypes, prejudice and resistance from subordinates, colleagues and superiors who were largely male, which made matters worse.

The intense scrutiny senior women face by virtue of being the only woman at that level puts huge pressure on them. And as we discussed in the last chapter, it also forces them to continue playing by the rule book of stereotypes that has been crafted for them by men. Prof. Kanter says, 'For token women, the price of being one of the boys is a willingness to turn occasionally against the girls. Put up or shut up is a way of going along to get along because noise is trouble.'

These are not mere consequences of a high-pressure job. These are the consequences of being a *woman* holding a high-pressure job. Being the only woman in the room, dealing with the prejudices stemming from being the only woman in the room and then having no one to share that experience with compounds the isolation that senior women feel.

Research on loneliness reveals that it is as lethal as smoking fifteen cigarettes a day! Isolation will not only wreck our mental health, but it will also create havoc with our physical health as well.

So we have no choice, ladies. We have to become proactive, look for our version of Wonder Woman's Themyscira and create communities from scratch if we have to. We urgently need to do this not only to battle the loneliness we feel but also to break free of the stereotypical roles and outmoded notions we are expected to abide by.

When I was running Radio City, I was the only woman in the boardroom, as usual, among a bunch of grave and sombre financial investors. (No, their demeanour wasn't anything to do with our performance; we were rocking the radio industry. It was just their default disposition!) One day, just as a meeting was about to begin, one of them started to whisper to me hoarsely, 'RSVP! RSVP!' I couldn't understand either his peculiar code or his sudden compulsion for secrecy, so bluntly and rather loudly I inquired, 'What's RSVP, Anil?' 'Royal Strap Visible Please,' he responded, red-faced, pointing to an errant bra strap visible on my shoulder.

Though momentarily discomfited, I later had a good laugh with him over the fact that while he seemed to know the intimate acronyms convent girls use, I had no clue about them! Once back in my own office however, I wondered how differently such a situation would have been handled if another woman had been in the room with me. For one, no female colleague would have been driven into an apoplectic fit over a peeking strap like men seem to be, and for another, an eyebrow would have been raised, a signal understood and a surreptitious adjustment made without anyone being the wiser!

In creating communities, we will find the power to be ourselves. But traditionally, social spaces have been designed for men – golf courses, bars and exclusive clubs a la *Mad Men* – and they remain largely and stubbornly true to these historical legacies. Women who have wanted to leverage the power of sisterhood have been held back by the sheer lack of spaces to convene and converge. But today we can create our own space on social media, a powerful and accessible platform. The best example in recent times of the intersection of social media and sisterhood has been the #MeToo movement. It is a reminder of our strength, of the fact that when women actively reach out to form a coven, not only do we find support but we also drive change.

For a woman sitting at home and feeling angry about the injustice committed against her, it need not be a lonely moment any longer. She can talk about it on social media and she will find support and encouragement. Magically, this also bolsters the courage of other women to come forward and share their stories of harassment at the hands of the same man! Together the survivors experience redemption through their sisterhood.

Whether it is sharing #MeToo stories or creating groups sharing the same interests like WOW-Women On Wanderlust or the hundred sarees campaign, social media has spread its tentacles so far and wide and deep that you can find a sister in support whatever your unique specifications may be.

Sometimes when I am fed up of being surrounded by men, more men and so many men around me, I imagine myself in an all-girls' commune somewhere far away on an island full of light and fresh air. I fantasise about how nimble I would feel – having shed all the layers of pretence and artifice along with the coatings of forbearance and resignation with which I arm myself on a daily basis to navigate the world of men.

I imagine this retreat to be like Themyscira, the island home of superhero Wonder Woman and the Amazons. Warriors of fearsome strength and valour, these women live together, fight together and swear to die together. They have no need to subvert or undermine themselves. They are free to embrace their power. They are all sisters who fly together on shared wings of openness and authenticity.

But we forget. We have no need of the mythological Themyscira or to escape into whimsical flights of fantasy. We have all the power we need right here. We have each other. We just need to make the effort to find our way to each other, to be there for each other and to support each other through thick and thin.

Whether you've been friends since nursery or have only met a few months ago at the yoga class or follow each other on Twitter, mark out your soul sisters and create your own circle of magic with them. Find the time to invest in these relationships not only for their sake but also for yours! I know you are brave and strong. You wouldn't have got where you are without these attributes. But equally you don't need to fight the good fight alone. Especially since so many of your soul sisters are forlornly flying around just as lonely as you are, looking in life's jigsaw for that corner in which to fit themselves and find anchor.

Alternatively, you can start smoking fifteen cigarettes a day and hope for temporary succour!

IN SHORT

- Working women face an uphill task every single day in trying to achieve desired business outcomes while fighting against a prejudiced social order and navigating inherently male-dominated ecosystems.
- The intense scrutiny senior women face by virtue of being the only woman at that level also puts huge pressure on them.
- The only way to manage this stress is to find like-minded women and create a support system around yourself.
- By investing in these relationships, you will find power and succour and help to create the change you seek.

Real-Life Role Models

What's the point of winning awards citing you as a powerful
woman if you don't empower other women?

—Arundhati Bhattacharya

When I was six, my mother asked me what I wanted to be when I grew up. 'Mother Teresa,' I replied, gazing at her solemnly. Lest you believe I was a child prodigy with a heart of gold or even worse, a precocious and dreadfully prissy little girl, let me assure you I was not. But my sentiment was innocent, sincere and heartfelt.

I did not grow up to become a selfless charitable woman who spends all her waking hours taking care of the underprivileged. I am an honourable capitalist and driving the P&L (profit and loss) of my organisation is important to me. I enjoy wealth creation for myself and for all my stakeholders. But in keeping with my childhood ambitions, I have always looked for opportunities to create impact in whatever way I can. So while my fantasies have been slightly grand – I become a strict principal roaming around with a scowl and a cane in my hands – in reality I have tried to be a teacher and mentor wherever possible. As a happy consequence of being in leadership positions since the age of twenty-three, I have had several opportunities to mentor and guide women either in my own organisations or elsewhere. And over the course of numerous conversations with them, I have come to the conclusion that there is a crying need for more women role models to help these young women navigate the unchartered territories of public spaces.

Women are flooding into the workplace in India in unprecedented numbers today. Many of them are the first generation of women in their families to work. They have fought courageously with parents and in-laws for the right to work. Every single day they withstand tremendous personal pressure just so they have the freedom to earn a living.

However, when they enter the workplace and look around, 95 per cent of the leaders they see are male. This triggers two thoughts in the subconscious mind of these young women. The first is the conclusion that 'leader equals male', so naturally a woman cannot aspire to be a leader. And secondly, they implicitly see a biased environment and probably demur from having conversations about the challenges they face at work with male supervisors. That's not because male leaders are any less receptive than female ones. It's because they innately identify with the latter and feel intimidated by the former. Consequently, they will either underperform or after a point, leave that organisation.

What the scarcity of role models can do to a generation was driven home to me while listening to an episode of Malcolm Gladwell's *Revisionist History* podcast. In the episode titled 'Miss Buchanan's Period of Adjustment', Gladwell deconstructs the consequences of the US Supreme Court's landmark 1954 ruling ending segregation in schools.

While the Brown v. Board of Education ruling marked the end of separate schools for white and black children and was hailed as a great victory against racism, it ironically rang a death knell for black teachers. As schools began to be integrated, teachers in massive numbers had to be let go since many weren't required. And while society was finally willing to allow black and white children to be educated together, it was yet to reach the stage where parents were okay with black teachers educating white students. As a consequence, most of the teachers who were let go were black.

What no one paid attention to was how this would affect the black students. Robbed of teachers who were like them, and more importantly, understood them, the performance of black students plummeted. Top-performing black students from previously segregated schools became mediocre or below average. Their graduation rates, chances of following through with higher education and moving up in life was so severely negatively affected that even now, seventy years later, they have been unable to catch up!

Having role models is the biggest and most important driver of diversity. When people ask me what I have done in my own organisations to ensure diversity, my immediate response is that the only thing I have done is ensure there are enough senior women around!

A woman will stay on in an organisation when she sees senior women around her because this sends out several subconscious messages to her. She feels empowered thinking that if they could do it, so can she. She feels that it is a safe place for women. She is excited to dream about reaching the level she sees other women attain in that workplace. She tacitly believes that the organisation has no inherent gender biases because it has people like her in senior roles.

If you are a senior woman in your organisation, you should use your hard-won position to not only right the wrongs done to you but also ensure these wrongs don't happen to young women entering the workforce today. That can only happen when you play a visible role in the workplace. To build each other up, we have to invest long-term sustained efforts in coaching and mentoring women leaders of tomorrow. Cloistering ourselves in an ivory tower with that 'Power Woman' award is an exercise in self-aggrandisement and nothing else.

Let me share what a study produced jointly by the Geena Davis Institute on Gender in Media and the J. Walter Thompson Company has to say. It revealed that female role models in film and TV are hugely influential in driving women to improve their lives. In the study, 90 per cent of women from across the globe said they felt that female role models in film and TV have been hugely impactful in their lives.

What Indian films and TV have to offer little girls was revealed to me through a dreadful example. While visiting a friend, the five-year-old daughter of her house help offered to entertain us with her dance moves. We readily agreed. What followed horrified me worse than the scariest movies I'd ever seen.

The little girl gyrated her breasts and hips while crooning the seductive refrain of the latest chart-topping item number. She had no idea of the meaning behind what she was singing or the moves she was making while dancing, but was confident that this was what she was supposed to be doing.

A study by IBM looked at movies made over fifty years in Bollywood to identify biases. It confirmed the largely decorative status of women in films. It also found that male characters had profession-driven roles with their occupations ranging from scientist and army general to singer and professor. Meanwhile the women characters were appearance- or relationship-driven. For the handful of women characters who had any profession, it was restricted to teaching and secretarial roles.

Our boys grow up seeing themselves as doctors, CEOs and presidents. Our girls grow up thinking they are worth only the contextual roles defined by their relationships – mother, daughter, wife, etc. By the time they enter the workforce, much of the damage has already been done. When they see men occupy the majority of leadership positions, it only emphasises the truth of their early socialisation. That power means male. That they are destined to play forever the supporting cast – a Mona darling, the sidekick of an all-powerful gangster or a wheelchair-bound sister to showcase the nurturing 'family' side of the hero!

It is thus even more important that the women I am talking to in this book stand up and be counted as role models. The presence of strong role models in an organisation will give rise to a host of new archetypes our young ladies can aspire to play – the legal eagle, the iron lady, the prudent financial controller or the collaborative manager. The lack thereof will leave them reconciling to the stereotypical and submissive roles of supportive secretary or glamorous receptionist.

Young women look to us for guidance, experience-backed wisdom and for that silver bullet that helped us reach wherever we have. As senior women it is our job to help decode those steps for them. Especially when we know they are being pressurised by society to play passive and secondary roles.

Madeleine Albright rightly said, 'There is a special place in hell for women who don't help other women.' So reach out and pull them up behind you. But while doing so, definitely remember to tell them that, once upon a time, you too were just like them.

Rajeshwari, a young woman working in a new-age housing company, came to me lacking in confidence and raw in experience. But she was burning with ambition to grow. She had sought me out after a lecture I had given at CII as part of their women-empowerment programme.

You could make out that she was from a very middle-class family and had to really push against the pressures of her conventional upbringing, both to educate herself in the first place and then to ensure she continued working. Through the duration of our monthly mentoring sessions, I witnessed her rapid progress and growth into a great accountant and professional.

Despite a poor start in life and constant pressure at home from her unemployed husband and domineering mother-in-law to give up her job and start a family, she showed indomitable willpower and remained focussed on her job. One day while discussing some of the problems holding her back at home, I casually mentioned how I had been elbow-deep in dirty utensils when she had called me at home the previous evening.

She looked flabbergasted. 'Madam, what are you saying?' she squeaked. 'You wash dishes?' 'Yes, when I don't have help at home!' I said. That domestic troubles befell me too and I had to clean dirty dishes made her feel far closer to me than all the talks we'd shared through the months about upskilling, widening her understanding of finance and business, and her own personal problems!

She left our session that day with the unshakeable belief that I was a kindred spirit. Her ambition was bolstered by the fact that she could see in me a little bit of herself.

One of the less vocalised worries plaguing younger women is that the lives of successful women who came before them have been easier than their own. They see the martinis and the foreign holidays and are convinced that these women had certain exclusive opportunities available to them, which helped them succeed.

Not only is this thought scary but also very overwhelming. So much so that many young women feel unequal to climbing those Olympian heights where all their goddesses reside. The biggest disservice we will do to younger women is to perpetuate this belief further.

Let's shatter this corrosive thought and pound it out of their hearts and minds. That is the best way we can empower them and that should be our foremost legacy to them – I am just like you. See my roughened hands from all that scrubbing. And if I could do it, so can you! After all, being a role model is not about being an inspiration. It's about being an aspiration.

IN SHORT

- One of the best ways you can support the cause of gender diversity is by becoming a role model yourself.
- Young women require visible role models to give them the confidence to aspire for more. You cannot let them down.
- But be a relatable role model. Show them you are the same as them. If you present yourself as someone who is so special that no one can follow your path, you would have failed in this responsibility.

Menopause

*Change is disturbing when it is done to us,
exhilarating when it is done by us.*

—Rosabeth Moss Kanter

The insomnia came out of nowhere. I was forty-five when I suddenly stopped sleeping at night. While HD snored next to me, I spent my nights tossing and turning, the light bulb in my head stubbornly refusing to switch off. My nights were neatly sub-sectioned into phases of trying to sleep and falling asleep only to wake up feeling too hot or too cold, interspersed with hallucinatory moments of thinking that I had, against all odds, fallen asleep!

The stress from the lack of sleep made Swiss cheese of my brain. Previously acknowledged for my laser-sharp focus and eagle-like ability to swoop into the core of the issue, I found myself meandering about in a foggy and muddled mental state, making desperate attempts to camouflage the confusion in my mind from the troops.

For a number of years, I bounced like a yo-yo between sleeplessness-induced stress and stress-induced sleeplessness. I tried every cure, juggling allopathy and quack remedies, including sleeping pills, white noise apps, aromatherapy, oil-rubs, pillow sprays and magic potions straight out of the

Harry Potter books. Most male doctors either dismissed my concerns or misdiagnosed them.

Only a female doctor hit the nail on the head. She told me right away, 'This is the start of your perimenopause. Please be aware that you will go through these symptoms for quite some time, like five to seven years!'

I was stunned into silence. I had associated menopause with women in their late fifties and early sixties. While I didn't fancy myself a spring chicken, this stark reminder of ageing was a sudden and rude shock.

The body didn't care about my feelings on the matter. In the months and years that followed, I revolved in a whirlpool of mood swings, irritability, impulsiveness, abject pessimism and energetic enthusiasm. I was impatient, quick to anger and prone to making rash decisions. My once powerful memory bailed on me. Previously I'd fancied myself a heroic captain at work, managing my crew on the high seas. Now I felt the *Titanic* threatening to capsize on me.

It was now that an adolescent memory came to me unbidden. I recalled how my usually bright and cheerful mother would suddenly break into tears at all hours of the day. I didn't know what was happening and I don't think she did either. In the typical fashion of self-obsessed teenagers, I shrugged it off with a 'crazy grown-ups' eye-roll.

Now that I was facing this maddening metamorphosis myself I finally empathised with what she had gone through. When our mothers and grandmothers were going through menopause, they had two choices. Either to take it in their stride or to suffer in silence. They may have become gloomier, quieter or depressed. But they never asked for help. After all they had been conditioned since childhood not to call attention to their 'womanly' troubles.

Why am I calling attention to it now then? What place does a woman's reproductive health have in a book about career and leadership?

Many of you I am talking to are at the cusp of perimenopause and also overloaded with work in your professional capacities. This is really the first generation of women who will be working in substantial numbers in the public workspace while facing menopause. The majority of earlier generations of women going through menopause were housewives. Secondly, perimenopause is coming earlier than it did ever before. According to a study by the Institute for Social and Economic Change (ISEC), about 4 per cent of women between the ages of twenty-nine and thirty-four experience signs of menopause. The figure goes up to 8 per cent for women between the ages of thirty-five and thirty-nine!

Women going through menopause or perimenopause face added stressors today, which have greatly exacerbated the symptoms and degree of suffering they endure. In fact, menopause is being recognised as an emerging health crisis in India.

We will soon have a silent epidemic affecting a reasonably large chunk of our workforce, and we cannot afford not to talk about it. For all of you who have spent decades in building a thriving career and sterling reputation, the vagaries inflicted by menopause are likely to undo that hard work unless you know it is happening to you.

Ladies, if you want to achieve success in the workplace, there are certain life phases that will demand your dedication. Your willingness to work after marriage. Your willingness to balance work and parenting. And finally twenty years later, your ability to deal with menopause. Because we don't talk about it, read about it or even know about it, when the symptoms come out of the blue we don't know we should take it seriously. And worst of all, we give in to the raging hormonal impulses instead of fighting them.

There is nothing to panic about and of course you don't have to start preparing twenty years in advance. But you need to know that there is one more obstacle coming your way in case you think that you are done with all the challenges a working woman faces. Forewarned is forearmed.

I stared astonished at my friend Neelima as she detailed her new life plan to me when we bumped into each other at Khan Market. She, who had been a high-flying executive living in a plush Mumbai apartment with her husband and two children till yesterday, had become a free-ranging bird today. She announced she had separated from her husband and, at forty-eight, had moved to Delhi to live by herself.

I was shocked because I had always presumed theirs to be a happy marriage. She agreed, saying that they had been happy together. Her move was not precipitated by any problems or issues in their marriage. She had chosen to live alone suddenly, after almost three decades of marriage, because she wanted to 'discover' herself.

She shared that she had got married almost immediately after college. They had the usual spats and disagreements inherent to any marriage, but overall they had been good for each other. They'd raised two beautiful children together. But getting swept up in family life so young had left her no room to explore herself as an individual.

So she had quit Mumbai (and her marriage with it), shifted to Delhi and was living in a barsati (a small one-room rooftop apartment). I was perplexed. Barsatis look good in movies when they are used as a trope to show a young woman living the free life of her dreams, all bedecked with fairy lights (the barsati, not the heroine). But in real life, frankly, they are quite uncomfortable and grimy (which is why you need the fairy lights). I couldn't imagine living in a barsati at the age of even twenty, forget fifty! And my face, never my political ally in the best of times, must have shown my horror.

But she was unfazed. She was enjoying the freedom of living in an eight-by-ten feet room. Ironic, given her Mumbai flat was around five thousand square feet! Her children had grown up. She was exhilarated at having shrugged off all attachments and ridden off into the sunset by herself. I remained perplexed until it hit me that it was menopause talking.

Unfortunately, she was not the first friend of mine to make a rash life decision.

Around the same time, Sudha, a similarly aged friend, told me she had read whatever she could lay her hands on about menopause once her doctor had confirmed the symptoms. According to her, the physical and emotional metamorphosis of menopausal women was at par with the extreme changes undergone by adolescents during puberty – thanks to hormonal swings and imbalances in the body. Unfortunately, while we have all been so understanding of teenage angst, none of us acknowledges the issue of menopause, which being a specific 'womanly' problem has been conveniently swept under the carpet.

So Sudha had spectacularly decided to make dramatic changes in her life as commanded by the hormonal swings of menopause! She had been staying in the USA with her family for fifteen years. Her husband was completely Americanised and her daughter genuinely thought America

was home. But menopausal Sudha moved her family back
to India overnight.

Her sixteen-year-old daughter was devastated and was
literally counting the days until college when she would
go to an American university and never come back. Her
husband had no job in India. He worked with an American
firm remotely and thus had to adjust his entire schedule to
work at night. Their family life had completely gone out of
gear. But Sudha remained resolute.

'For twenty years I've done what they wanted to do.
Now they have to do what I want to do,' she insisted. 'But
you're harming your family, aren't you, by demanding this?' I
queried. 'So what? To deal with this difficult time in my life,
my chakras need to be on Indian soil for perfect alignment,'
she intoned.

While I am all for women empowerment and for us
taking ruthless control of our lives, I also wonder how
many of these words were hers and how much belonged
to her reading on menopause. She had devoured so much
on the condition that she was playing out what the books
told her to do.

The sheer variety of menopausal examples quite startled
me. There was my mother who had borne it in silence and
expected the same of me. There was my suddenly hippie
friend 'finding' herself in a barsati in Delhi. There was
my expat friend who had uprooted her family overnight
after fifteen years abroad. And then there was me. Sleep-
deprived, exhausted, hormonal me.

Menopause can create cataclysmic changes within all of
us. But because of ignorance and the lack of conversation
around it, there is nowhere for us to go and even understand
what is happening to us. All of us who were going through

this stage in our lives were desperately hoping to anchor ourselves and find meaning amid the chaos through different actions. Even the friends who had resorted to changing their lives overnight hoped to come to terms with what was happening to them through external changes. I don't know whether either of these women was doing the right thing. But I do know that major life changes are best not made in the midst of so much turbulence.

A single symptom of menopause can give rise to a host of new unrelated ones. If like me you suffer from sleeplessness, then know that insomnia leads to depression, cognitive impairment, irritability and even mild symptoms of PTSD. You are trapped in a vicious cycle of mood swings and unproductivity that feeds on your agony and creates more despair.

When you go through menopause, you will invariably also be dealing with other life changes. Whether you are facing bittersweet regrets or pondering over your mortality or simply experiencing the trauma of the empty nest, the physiological and philosophical cocktail you are subject to can be unpleasant at best and wrecking at worst.

No one would willingly choose the trial by fire that is menopause. But it is a process of transformation that all women have to go through, whether we like it or not.

Thus it is important to know that this will happen, and to read about it, prepare for it and talk about it. The one piece of advice I keep on reinforcing is to practise awareness and mind management. We have to recognise what is happening and link it to how we are feeling. Knowledge is empowering and critical in helping us make informed, reasoned choices instead of impulsive ones. Realisation precedes corrective action. And once you know, you can ensure you do whatever is possible to alleviate the trauma. Meditate. Exercise. Use the power of the sisterhood. Commiserate openly with your girlfriends. Share your problems with your family.

As an inveterate silver-lining advocate, I also believe that menopause is not gloom and doom alone. The one constant about change is that it always has an upside! And the big positive here is that with your testosterone increasing to male-like proportions, your confidence also shoots up to masculine heights! So instead of allowing menopause to play havoc with your emotions, you can and must channelise the self-assuredness it gives you to finally tell the world, your aunt, the nosy neighbour downstairs and your husband (the last one is optional): 'I really don't give a damn!' And mean it!

IN SHORT

- Among the many challenges and hardships women face in their adventures at home and work, there is one more looming on the horizon – menopause.
- Unfortunately, despite the intensity of changes it wreaks on women, it is a topic that has been kept well below the radar so far.
- It is important to understand its implications by reading and talking about it, so when it comes it is not an unexpected or alarming guest.
- Knowledge will help us deal with it better. Forewarned is forearmed.

Midlife Crisis

I live in that solitude which is painful in youth,
but delicious in the years of maturity.

—Albert Einstein

I was thirty-five the first time I was called 'Aunty'. I found that immensely funny. Maybe the boys who had shouted that word to me across the road while puffing up their chests to distract from their milk moustaches thought I deserved the label. Or maybe rating women into categories of desirability based on age was a sport that helped them feel more like men. Aunty is a much-maligned and pejorative term in our country, designed to summarily demote women from attractiveness to matronly-ness. However, it was like water off a duck's back at that time. I narrated the story to the girl-gang, we insouciantly shrugged it off our shapely shoulders and went about being our usual flamboyant selves.

In the preceding fifteen years I had built a fabulous life that I enjoyed immensely. I had resolutely scaled the evolutionary ladder from naïve teenager to confident senior leader one step at a time and didn't intend to look back. The mirror smiled at me lovingly every morning and the few lines on my face were cheerful crinkles rather than mature wrinkles, which I thought added great character and depth to my face! No street urchins were going to make me question how hot and happening I was.

Flash-forward a decade. Ranbir Kapoor walked into our studio one fine morning. The millennial heartthrob had come for interviews to promote his latest film and was immediately thronged by crowds of young women (and some men) desperate to inhale his essence. They accosted him to click selfies, that millennial version of autographs, and he pandered to all of them with good humour. He was introduced to me and while we were chatting, I found myself engulfed in a disconcerting feeling of maternal protectiveness! He reminded me of my son, even though he is a generation older. I worried that his last film hadn't done well and hoped that this one would be better. My tender heart rued how thin he seemed. I wondered whether he ate properly. I mentally castigated the film industry for expecting actors to starve for appearance's sake.

And that's when I suddenly realised I had become OLD! When earlier, proximity to a good-looking male would send several butterflies and a host of other woodland creatures fluttering in my stomach, today the only feeling that consumed me was motherly love!

A twenty-one-year-old Apurva or even the thirty-five-year-old Apurva who had laughed off being called an Aunty would never identify with this crazy lady I had become, the one who just wanted to feed the movie star in her office a hearty Punjabi meal. The collision that is the reckoning with one's midlife occurred at full force for me in that moment. I realised that unbeknown to all of us, the girl-gang had transmogrified almost overnight into a version of my mom's lady friends!

Horrified, I noticed we were spending our entire lunch sessions either commiserating over subtle but certainly not imperceptible signs of ageing or discussing various illnesses real and imagined, much like the women at mom's kitty-party sessions, which end up being a virtual trip through a medical clinic!

The immutable fact about middle age is that no one is immune to it. Maybe it will be a slow dawning of truth for you. Or maybe, as in my case, it will be a sudden explosion that hits you unexpectedly.

While midlife issues are gender agnostic, arguably women have it worse. While men supposedly age like fine wine, we are considered crinkly crones by forty. Nearly four generations of heroines were deemed to have reached their dotage around their early thirties and retired accordingly, while our current crop of sixty-something heroes continue to romance the latest twenty-one-year-old entering the movie industry.

Being confronted with one's mortality is never pleasant. Dealing with the psychological attack on our self-worth while also fielding the existential crises that are sure to descend around this time is daunting. Added to that is the onset of perimenopause, which we just discussed. Cue the cascade of regrets, nostalgia, what-ifs and if-onlys.

Men suffer from midlife crises just as much as women do. But they deal with it far better, give or take a few tattoos, leather jackets, motorbikes and flirtations with twenty-six-year-old PYTs (pretty young things). And that's because men manage to retain their sense of selfhood, through the turmoil of work, marriage and child-rearing, while women completely immerse themselves in these tasks.

We juggle being good wives, mothers and professionals. We rush home from the office to oversee homework and organise playdates and rush back again to finish the project report on time. We make sure the kitchen cupboards are stocked with food when we go away on work trips, including labelled meals and refrigerated parathas.

We baulk at the pressure and dream of solo getaways where all we will do is drink cocktails on the beach, dressed in wispy (albeit non-revealing) resort wear! We fantasise about eating meals that we didn't need to shop, cook or plan for. But as we discussed earlier in the book, secretly we love being needed this much. We enjoy the feeling that everything will fall apart if not for our herculean management skills – both at home and in the office. And though we miss the person we used to be before being drowned by responsibilities, we don't grudge the sacrifices because of the joy this brings us.

And then suddenly that life as we knew it is gone. The change takes effect gradually but the realisation hits us like the bucket of ice water that those ALS challenge participants doused themselves with to participate in the viral internet challenge. The marriage has settled into a comfortable harmony that no longer needs conscious upkeep. The children have grown up and moved out. The career has achieved a level of success we could once only dream of.

We now have in our grasp that holy grail that seemed too fantastical to be true – time for ourselves. Yet when the key expectations and duties that defined our lives for so long are no longer present, our first reaction isn't happiness or relief. It's a sinking feeling of emptiness. When this empty-nest syndrome strikes, men continue to have their hobbies and interests and friends to turn to. We don't even remember what ours had been in the first place. Consequently, the desolation becomes inescapable.

But it doesn't have to be this way. A temporary mourning period is acceptable. Lamenting the emptiness and wallowing in suffering as a way of life is not. Life is asking us to reboot, but sometimes we are too stuck to move. When my son moved away from home, I too experienced the gut-punching pain that comes with the wrenching of a family nucleus. Of course I was reassured that some things will never change when the next month said son landed back home carrying bags of dirty clothes to be laundered, all the while announcing how independent he now was.

But I digress.

My own reboot was baby steps at first. A theatre date with the hubby, a hangout session with a dearly loved but not oft seen friend. Gradually as I felt life seep back into previously ignored corners, I was energised enough to kick things up a notch. I reconnected with old school friends. Fortunately, there are no outside witnesses to our meetups where fifty-year-old women squeal and giggle like tweens and call each other 'girlie'.

Then came the crown jewel experience of my life reboot – a solo trip. Three days of wining and dining by myself at a resort. It was not so much the physical luxury as it was the emotional space to rediscover who I was when I was not being a wife, mother or boss. I finally realised why *Eat Pray Love* has become such a cult hit with middle-aged women. Spending time with yourself is addictive. Once you start, it's a habit you will keep going back to.

It's okay at this stage to be a teensy weensy bit more selfish and to put your needs first. It is critical to do a lot more self-care. It can be disciplined self-care like being conscious of what you are eating and exercising daily to help with hormone regulation. It can be indulgent self-care like weekly spa days or taking weekend trips on your own for some 'me time'. It could even be learning to fight for the remote or learning to say NO loudly and clearly! 'Please note I am going to watch *GoT* and not the hundredth version of a cricket league!' 'I do not want to eat what you decide to order.' 'I will keep the curtains drawn and the AC at sub-polar temperatures should I elect to.' 'And I will certainly not get up and start organising lunch the second I have sat down to read the papers just because you are hungry!' Aah, the freedom of saying NYET!

It's also okay to finally and totally stop giving a damn! Your best friend may point out that you have added yet another tire around the midriff; the sleazy neighbour will continue to talk to your décolleté rather than to you; husband dearest will be astounded that the fridge is not stocked with his favourite beer, despite the fact that you have been travelling on work the entire week; any of these things would have had you tearing your hair out or over-compensating defensively in your manic thirties. But now you just couldn't be bothered. 'And here's how my middle finger looks, dear neighbour,' you may say in a very ladylike manner (Rhett Butler would be proud of you)!

Most importantly, it is okay to accept that you don't need to be the adept multitasker you have been all your adult life. Now is the time for you to free up your plate, delegate responsibilities and live every single moment precisely the way you choose to do so.

One of my pals, Nidhi, had an epiphany in her mid-forties when it dawned on her that she had spent a lifetime accumulating expensive Kanjeevarams but had never had enough time to attend occasions that could justify wearing one. Faced with a cupboard full of beautiful but unworn

Kanjeevarams, she decided to do something about it. She started wearing her Kanjeevarams to office. Every day at 9 a.m. she would walk into the office and bedazzle everyone, decked out like Rekha at the Filmfare Award functions! We adored her for her savoir-faire and carpe-diem-ness and were much inspired by her.

We have all spent the first forty-five years of our lives accruing security and stability while fulfilling all the roles demanded from us. In this first phase of our lives we burdened ourselves with expectations, imposed as much by others as our own selves. Let's spend the next forty-five years having fun and doing only those things that we choose to. Now, which Kanjeevaram will you wear tomorrow?

IN SHORT

- Midlife crises for women are far more painful than for men, because they come with other life changes like an empty nest and menopause.
- But this can also be a great time to reboot and rediscover yourself.
- Finally your responsibilities of bringing up your children (and husband) are over and you can concentrate on yourself.
- Use this time to rediscover and re-ignite your passions and make choices that appeal only to you.
- At this stage in your life, you have the self-confidence, the maturity (and the money and the time) to know and do what you want. So get, set and zoom away into the horizon of your choice!

Somebody's Something

She's always been somebody's something.
She's been everything but alone.
A daughter, a lover, a wife, and a mother –
She's lived every life but her own.
She'd say, 'That's just called being a woman.'
She's always been somebody's something.
She wonders what it might be like to be somebody else.
She wonders what it'd feel like to be free.
When she tries to imagine being nobody's nothing,
That's someone she'd never want to be.

—Kaci Bolls

When I proudly sent the very first copy of my book *Lady, You're Not a Man!* to my mother, she looked at it, then immediately called me up and aggrievedly asked why her name was not there! Since the book was prominently dedicated to her, I was a bit taken aback. 'But look at the first page, Momsie – you are right there,' I said in a mildly exasperated tone. I could hear the turning of pages over the phone and then a few moments later she muttered crossly, 'But it just says "To Mummy" … Where is my name?'

And so it is for all women. Our entire life gets telescoped into one brief appellation, and just like that, in a jiffy, we are reduced to merely being somebody's something.

Tinku's mummy and Raju's sister and Mrs Khanna and the daughter-in-law of that nasty Mrs Bhatia who lives in 504. It almost seems that we have no identity of our own except as an appendage to a man!

Even our family name is not ours to own forever and must fall by the wayside as we adopt our husband's name after marriage. Or we can choose to sound very splendid and roam the earth with a double-barrelled Smythe-Winston or Kapur-Sud title. I assure you that brings its own set of challenges however, and is not something I would recommend since it also comes accompanied by unwarranted and repetitive explanations to be given to the passport officer, the electricity company and the Aadhar card system, which asks us rather nosily to explain why we have a surname that is different from our husband/father/ son's name. Thus all it ends up being is a very grand but meaningless (and painful) gesture to defy the patriarchal order!

The loss of a name is mere semantics at the end of the day; after all a rose by any other name smells just as sweet, as the great bard wrote so many years ago. The much bigger loss for women is the forfeiture of individuality that takes place after they get married. The transition from Miss Swaminathan to Mrs Shankar is more than a name change; it is like sloughing off old skin and with it, discarding childhood friends, city, hobbies, TV habits and sometimes, painfully, even family! A woman is the paraya dhan after all and must transform, at the cost of her personality, into a new avatar that has very little in common with who she was pre the one 'chutki sindoor'!

But you are no longer the coy bride of two decades ago and today I am talking to the poised, smart and self-assured woman who has recently and bravely dealt with: 1) the morphing of a sweet little baby who loved her mom into a sulky teenager who bangs doors and scowls like someone from *Assassin's Creed*, 2) being called aunty by the cute neighbour, 3) working with insolent millennials who were born exactly at the moment you were getting your first salary check and who keep reminding you about it – 'What is a fax, ma'am? ... You didn't have Google? How did you find out things? ... Wow! You were born in 1978? That's around Partition, isn't it ma'am? How cool! Did you know Gandhi-ji?'

And having dealt with these life-changing events with immense verve and flair (and reached thus far in the book) I want to invite you now to the post-interval stage in which you prepare yourself to soar to even further heights, above and beyond the limits of your imagination, and see for yourself what you are truly capable of!

So let's begin the pre-take-off prep.

Step one and the single-most important thing to do at this juncture is to rediscover and reclaim your lost self. Who were you before the layers of daughter, mother, wife, boss accumulated on you as time went by? What did you smile about when you were young? Do you remember what brought a frown on your face? Did you like dance or poetry or just the adda that happened in the evening near the building gate?

This is the moment you look into the mirror and reacquaint yourself with that stranger you see there. And when you stare closely at that image, you will realise that not only have you forgotten who she was, but she is also coated with so many artificial layers that you will have to actually excavate the real person that lies beneath, section by section. So go ahead, take a hard brush and exfoliate the residue of the struggles, the hardships, the criticisms and the compliments. Figure out what you believe in and stand for without the pressure of ambient prejudices. And get in touch with your unvarnished spirit and your core essence.

It is supremely difficult to do that, I assure you, to hear again that forgotten voice from a distant past, to see yourself as an individual, to drown out the cacophony of expectations. But only when you do that will you start revealing the unashamed, unapologetic, phenomenal and beautiful person underneath.

My sister-in-law Raksha was once a glamourous globe-trotting air hostess. She gave up her job and her creative outlets when she married my engineer brother-in-law. He was building an engineering firm from scratch and she joined him in his efforts to build his business. For thirty years she served as his right-hand person, managing the firm along with him despite having no interest in this technical field.

Raksha never grudged the work nor shouted from the rooftops about her sacrifice. She enjoyed being her husband's partner and was proud of having created a successful business with him. But the day their two children began working in the family firm, she walked away from it.

She announced to us that she had done her duty. Now it was time for her to focus on her own interests. She was going to explore her creativity in full force. She had always been interested in fashion and grooming. Apparel and textiles were of particular interest to her and in the hardcore engineering works that had surrounded her for so long, their colours and textures had faded into sepia tones. But now she was determined that she would go back and bring them to fruition. Within months she had sourced a set of artisan women from Hubli in Karnataka, worked with them to create intricately embroidered sarees and was soon ready with her first exhibition!

The family turned up in full support to attend her show and we were all completely impressed by what she had managed to achieve in such a short time and the fun she was having while fulfilling her heart's desire. After the event, I stayed back to help her fold the few sarees that had been left unsold, but she wouldn't let me touch them. She lovingly caressed each one, crooning to them like they were her offspring, gently swishing them this way and that until she was surrounded by expertly folded piles. She confessed to me that she felt each of the sarees had a personality of its own, centred on the old artisans who had lovingly and diligently embroidered them, and that she sometimes even talked to them! I rolled my eyes, laughing at her exaggerated romanticism, but felt hugely proud of her and the dramatic volte-face she had accomplished. From running an engineering company to becoming a successful creative designer!

Her journey should be the journey of each of us, where in the second phase of our lives, only we have a lien over its course and its path. This phase of our lives is about us. About our growth, our evolution and advancement – and it should be in the direction we wish it to be and at the pace we want to drive it at.

We have reached thus far by dint of immense hard work and perseverance. We have become successful entrepreneurs, senior lawyers, managers running not-for-profit organisations, school principals and marquee investment bankers. We may choose to do a 360-degree turn and take our life in another direction, or we may choose to continue on the same path with renewed vim and vigour; the vital thing to remember is that this is just the halfway mark. We have accomplished but a fraction of what we are truly capable of doing.

But for that we need to accept the challenge of becoming once more the best version of our new self and invoke the leader within!

To become the leader of your destiny, of your organisation or of yourself however, requires certain traits that you need to cultivate and develop. To know what those are, you must read on, my dear …

Picture abhi baaki hai, mere dost!

IN SHORT

- For the first half of our lives, most of us have been an addendum to our fathers, brothers, spouses and sons. It is now time to reclaim our lost identity.
- This mid-point in our lives comes with opportunities to make choices that are not dependent on the people around us.
- It is an opportunity to uncover our lost individuality, rejuvenate that essential self and start the journey towards building its best version, answerable to no one but ourselves.

PART TWO

Out of every one hundred men, ten shouldn't even be there,
eighty are just targets, nine are the real fighters,
and we are lucky to have them, for they make the battle.
Ah, but the one, one is a warrior, and he will bring the others
back.

—Heraclitus

Tough Love

Everything depends on upbringing.

—Leo Tolstoy, *War and Peace*

As a lady boss – whether you are running your own clinic or investment firm, or you are managing your family and their crazy schedules with the savoir-faire of a general while dealing with thousands of employees in your organisation – you need to have a specialised toolkit at your command to become a spectacular leader and manager. You certainly don't want to settle for anything less than being spectacular. After all you are not just any leader. You are the boss lady!

So in this part of the book, I want to share with you some nuggets of wisdom I have gathered along the way up my own career ladder. These are stories of building high-value organisations one patient brick at a time, of putting together talented players and teaching them to behave like a team. They are tales of setting grand strategies at the start of a year while never forgetting that the execution is just as important. They tell you that having a macro-perspective is a great leadership trait (and kudos to you for being such a visionary), but the job gets done only when you get the plumbing right, and the pipes and drains all clean and working. In this part we discuss that to succeed you need to have passion for the task and compassion for people in equal measure, and manoeuvring and balancing both these critical facets are the biggest challenges you will face every single day of your managerial life. So let's begin, as they say, at the very beginning.

I don't know whether you have noticed, but leadership is having its moment currently and everyone and their aunt wants to tell you what they think they know about it. It's very much like having a point of view on cricket; whether we know anything about the sport or not, every one of us 1.2 billion Indians has an opinion on the India vs Pakistan series, Sachin's finest innings or who was the better captain – Sourav, Dhoni or Kohli. The topic of leadership is a bit like that, and every senior manager who has been a CEO, ex-CEO, or an almost-CEO, and is obviously of the masculine gender and thus prone to pontificate, can give you the lengthier version of a TED talk on his personal opinion on leadership before you have so much as smiled at him prettily.

I am a lady boss however, and you all know that a no-nonsense, practical and sensible approach to leadership is our default style. We don't preach or sermonise. We don't stand up on platforms (in any case I have vertigo and two-inch platform heels are the best I can manage) and hold forth grandiosely. Instead we give pithy tips and subtle suggestions to stimulate everyone around us to think, and our leadership lessons are drawn not from the majestic high ground of theoretical thought, but from the minutiae of everyday living.

Precisely because these lessons are from the perspective of ground zero, where the real job of living and managing gets conducted, I believe they are all the more effective and also easy to apply. Indeed, one of the most important leadership lessons I learnt quite early on and constantly propagate is from the arduous yet oddly satisfying business of being a parent.

I offer this thought to you – that if you can get the core of parenting right, which is essentially to convert that little angel who is pulling at your dress and throwing a tantrum just as you are leaving for an already-overdue appointment, into a decent human who will be kind, polite and make a meaningful contribution to society, you have already learnt all that is required to be a good leader. Parenting, with its tear-your-hair-out moments interspersed with bouts of uncertainty at the lousy job you are doing and sprinkled with itsy-bitsy crumbs of smugness at those rare intervals when that little person is behaving well, is where you learn the vital art of leading. If you have understood that, I would almost dare suggest that you don't need to read this book any further! But never mind me, do carry on.

The essence of leadership in its basic, primal form, stripped of all jargon and affectation, is the ability to impact people's lives and help transform them into better and more productive professionals and human beings. Whether you are an entrepreneur running a small firm with three employees or a lawyer with just one clerk in attendance or the head of a mammoth MNC with a million employees spread across the world, the core of leadership is about positively influencing people and helping transform them into their best versions.

Now re-read the last sentence. How is that different from parenting, except that parenting entails a life-long commitment in comparison?

I remember in the initial days of setting up Radio City, while we were evolving the basic foundation of the

organisation we were trying to build, we conducted a
workshop with a leading HR firm to develop the values
that would define our culture.

As is their wont, the HR firm organised multiple
exercises designed to help us get in touch with our inner
selves and ascertain what our organisational vision would
be. The exercises included colourful balloons and myriad
hats, whiteboards and team spirit, and yards of green twine
with large nails attached at regular intervals, whose purpose
I still haven't fathomed since we didn't get around to
using it. We all earnestly got into the spirit of creating the
VMV (vision-mission-value) statement, which would be the
defining lodestar for the company for many years to come.

The workshop progressed along expected lines, several
HR truisms being volleyed about with great enthusiasm.
I particularly remember 'innovation led', 'people focused',
'process driven', 'customer first' being used repeatedly and
vociferously. It always impresses me that all good HR
trainers have the uncanny ability to channel the spirit of
childish enthusiasm and boundless eagerness even in the
most hardened executive or cynical loner in a team.

As the workshop progressed, I stopped the trainer
midway and firmly told him that one of the values that
I most certainly wanted to make part of the Radio City
culture was tough love. He gawked at me in utter disbelief.
If my memory serves me right, he goggled too. Then he led
me to the side of the room and in a horrified undertone
informed me that tough love was not 'corporate' enough to
be used as a value. With its parenting subtext, it just did
not have the seriousness or solemnity an organisational
value required. According to him, all VMV statements
had to be explicitly stuffed with gravitas and had to have

a minimum of fifteen words with multiple prefixes and suffixes to communicate their importance. This was no child's play after all, he expostulated. I wanted to point to the clown's hat he was wearing while giving me this lecture, but since he was on the verge of an apoplectic fit, I desisted. The poor chap's internal wires had already started a-twisting and a-turning in shame at the blasphemous thought of seeing 'Tough Love' painted graphically on our corporate corridors and on our coffee mugs!

But I persisted, and as you read more of this book it will gradually dawn upon you that perseverance is one of the virtues I am particularly fixated on. So naturally, tough love did become one of the values that Radio City practises even to this day.

Now you may ask why I was so keen to make tough love a core value at Radio City.

One of the most challenging struggles we face in our journey to become good leaders is to find the ideal mix between discipline and empathy or between managing processes and managing people. Every stage in the leadership pipeline is fraught with the danger of upsetting the delicate balance that is required between being people-oriented and result-focused. Or between caring and outcome. The equilibrium can be destabilised at an organisational level when budget cuts have to be enforced, which could potentially mean retrenching employees who have worked in the organisation for years. It can happen at an individual level when a sales executive misses his targets because of issues in his personal life. How does the manager balance the P&L and the person sitting across the table? Is it okay to miss sales numbers? Or frankly, should it not matter a damn that the employee's wife is sick and the only thing that should be seen while admonishing him are the quarter's unachieved numbers?

I had suggested 'Tough Love' to our trainer simply because applying this particular parenting principle to many such difficult situations has made them far easier for me to deal with. Isn't it a fact that if your child is throwing a tantrum or refusing to eat his food, or behaving in an atrociously impolite manner with your neighbours' aunt, you will discipline him, scold him or send him to stand in a corner? He knows what he has done is wrong and that you are punishing him for a particular misdeed. He also knows that despite being punished, he is loved and cared for. Indeed, because he is loved, he is being disciplined. And that's how parents practise tough love!

Similarly, managers need to be tough when performance is being discussed, while making every effort to ensure that the employee is being treated empathetically. They have to know the vital difference between judging a task and not the person, and censure the act and not the actor. If passion for excellence and compassion for people can coexist and work in tandem in a managerial operating style, there is no better demonstration of great leadership. People are not fools, and your team member will recognise that you are giving her feedback only to help her improve. She knows you value her and care about her, and that is the conscious effort you have to make in the tough love style of management.

Being a parent or a leader is not a test of popularity. It is a solemn duty we all have, a commitment we make that whoever passes through our circle of influence – our children, our executives or our managers – will become better at what they are doing through a series of interventions, some pleasant and some not so. If we have to be good leaders, tough choices have to be made and disagreeable calls need to be taken. Leadership is not a congeniality contest after all. But if we can do so with our humaneness intact, with our mind driven by results and our heart filled with empathy for people, parenting would have taught us a valuable lesson in management indeed!

IN SHORT

- One of the best places to learn leadership skills is the parenting academy, which teaches tough love.
- The principles of tough love include knowing when to discipline your child so that they grow up to be a better human being while reinforcing your love for them at all times so they are never in doubt that you care. This ensures that they understand your desire to improve them is because you value them. These are the same principles you need to apply at work.
- Balancing performance orientation with empathy for people is the toughest synchronisation for a leader. Understanding the ethos of tough love will make the job simpler.

Taming the Underling

The measure of a man is what he does with power.

—Greek Proverb

A lady asked me the other day to help her figure out how parents can teach their children to manage a crisis. Her contention was that while practice is a great way to become perfect, crises by their very nature are one-off events and therefore no one can prepare anybody to manage them.

Most sensible parents, I told her, are aware that they can't protect their children always nor will they be around each time to deal with the crises their kids face. Thus one of the most important life skills they try to teach their offspring is resilience. We repeatedly drill into our child's head that they need to get up after a fall and ride that bicycle again, or reappear for the test they failed, or stay put in that first lowly job and gain experience, despite having graduated with honours. We pray and wish for our children not to stumble, but equally we teach them how to get up and run once again should they fall. But to teach them resilience, we first have to instil courage in them. We need to tutor them to have the resolve to take that exam again, the nerve to jump into the deep end of the pool, the determination to get up on that cycle despite the scraped knee.

As parents we know courage will be the only companion that will see our children through any period of stress and that is an important legacy we would like to leave with them.

Then why do so many managers, directly or invidiously, work at eroding the courage and confidence of their juniors? This is one problem that I have not been able to fathom even after thirty years of working. It is obvious to me that leaders will want to accomplish great things in life and the only way they can succeed is if their teams do well, which will happen only if the teams have the resilience to deal with the turbulence that they will face in their work, for which they need to have courage. Ergo, the first principle in being a successful leader is teaching the troops confidence! Then why do managers behave inappositely? Perplexing!

One of my batchmates, Vishal, narrated this interesting anecdote to me recently about his boss who is a very well-respected marketing guru. 'Come what may, Basu never ever has anything good to say about me,' he grimaced. 'Every time I go to him with a strategy, an idea or a plan, he dismisses it disdainfully, saying you can do better, son! And although several times we have ended up implementing exactly my suggestion, it is never acknowledged as such,' the litany continued. 'When I was younger, at every single appraisal session of mine, Basu would say, "You still have to mature as a marketeer. I can see you have potential, but you are not there as yet. Keep trying. Push yourself beyond the limited outlook you have currently."'

As we continued chatting, Vishal told me reflectively, 'Initially I was in awe of him and thought that he was pushing me to excel for my own sake. Then I realised several appraisal years later that I had become like the growth prospects of the Indian GDP; invariably the potential is there, but it never seems to be achieved! And once when I asked him what he thought I should do to improve, Basu had no specific or concrete suggestions to make! That's the day I realised that the problem was not with me but with him. Whatever I did, I would always remain the bridesmaid and never the bride with Basu, because he didn't want any of his juniors to grow.'

I could hear the despondency in Vishal's voice. I remembered how starry-eyed he had been as a young brand manager when he had first started working with Basu. Not only did he have the opportunity to work in one of the most marquee marketing organisations in the country but it was also with Basu, the company's much-lauded marketing head.

Many times we are dazzled by talented, charismatic and respected senior leaders and we feel the need to seek their approval precisely because of the aura surrounding them. We are so overawed with their personas that we don't even realise how they are slicing at our self-confidence one snarky comment at a time.

In our book club we recently discussed *The Little Prince* by Antoine de Saint-Exupéry.

There was widespread discussion around the interaction between the Little Prince and a fox he meets on his travels across the planets, and how the fox teaches the Little Prince about love, one of the most valuable lessons in the book.

'Come and play with me,' proposed the little prince. 'I am so unhappy.'

'I cannot play with you,' the fox said. 'I am not tamed.'

'Ah! Please excuse me,' said the little prince. But, after some thought, he added: 'What does that mean — "tame"?'

'It is an act too often neglected,' said the fox. 'It means to establish ties.'

'To establish ties?'

'Just that,' said the fox. 'To me, you are still nothing more than a little boy who is just like a hundred thousand other little boys. And I have no need of you. And you, on your part, have no need of me. To you, I am nothing more than a fox like a hundred thousand other foxes. But if you tame me, then we shall need each other. To me, you will be unique in all the world. To you, I shall be unique in all the world ...'

'I am beginning to understand,' said the little prince. 'There is a flower ... I think that she has tamed me ...'

And of course the message is about how by giving our time and our effort and our emotions to somebody, we build a special relationship with that person, and it is this love that makes each of us unique. But I have pondered on the use of the word 'taming' as a parallel for love and wondered whether there is an underlying cynicism in the context. Maybe the author is trying to tell us that often the reality is that we want to control the people we love. And that love is nothing but a desire for ownership. I think that is also the lesson in this tale, which is why it is considered not just a children's book but equally an important fable for adults.

I so wish that the current strong and mighty captains of industry would move their narcissistic gaze away from their own reflection and realise this. So many senior leaders I know behave in a manner calculated to reduce their juniors to timid, unsure professionals who will then remain perpetually dependant on their great leader to save their souls, shelter them and care for them. Leaders such as Basu believe that they know best and their disciples should follow them unwaveringly and steadfastly. And the price for their devotees' loyalty is the protection of the guru. Managers like him live in an imaginary land where they see themselves in technicolour glory striding across stormy deserts and choppy seas while their followers march singing *Chale Chalo* behind them for all eternity. It reminds me of the 'taming' the fox explains to the Little Prince.

But you are the new age leader who doesn't need to tame anyone or rely on only their loyalty to buoy you. You have confidence, intelligence and the self-assurance to deal with strong team players. More importantly, as a woman you understand the power of partnerships and of collaboration. You have successfully partnered with your husband and collaborated with parents and in-laws in raising your children. Since prehistoric days when your foremothers lived in caves, they understood the strength of the collective over the singular and the same ancient wisdom courses through your veins.

A leader is only as good as the team she has around her. And as leaders we need to have teammates who have intelligence and nerve standing beside us. The moment we teach courage to our team, we may also embolden them to question our judgement, to have opinions contrary to ourselves and to not think of us as demi-gods, which in any case we aren't. And that is perfectly fine. The advantages of diverse opinions and brave teammates far outweigh the disadvantages. I would trade an army of timorous followers for three brave warriors watching my back (though they may argue with me incessantly in private) any day!

IN SHORT

- Wise leaders understand the importance of having brave teammates around them, who have minds of their own.
- They encourage dissent in thinking so that the solutions that emerge have had the benefit of diversity.
- Thus courage is one of the primary skills they seek in their teams or strive to inculcate in them.
- As a boss lady, channel your inherent strength of nurturing and learn to be an enabling rather than a debilitating boss.

Good Leaders Are Great
Communicators

*The single biggest problem in communication is the illusion
that it has taken place.*

—George Bernard Shaw

If I asked for your definition of communication, what
would you say?

People of whom I've asked this question on multiple
occasions have come up with a plethora of rather interesting
responses. 'It is to outline a point to someone.' Bang on. 'The
way people speak with each other.' Right-o. 'It is talking.'
Beautifully simplistic. 'It is effectively telling people what
to do.' How very CEO of you.

I personally find the Oxford English Dictionary
definition of communication most elegant because it is
both short and to the point. Additionally, it is also highly
relevant to the modern business leader. Let's examine this
definition that describes communication as 'the successful
conveying or sharing of ideas and feelings.' The reason I find
this definition particularly pertinent is that it highlights
that communication is not only about transmission but
also about reception! In order for it to be classified as
communication, it needs to be *successfully* conveyed and

understood. Now tell that to Mr CEO who is very pleased with himself after a town hall where he droned on endlessly using the seventy-six multicoloured slides his executive assistant had prepared, of which only a fraction registered with his audience! Or the entrepreneur who presents a business plan to a potential investor in which every third word is an acronym specific to his industry. The dazed look your investor is giving you is not from admiration at your vision, my dear, but because he is still trying to make sense of this: 'So the moment we have 35 per cent of our ACK in place, we would have delivered an innovative PBX solution to the customer acquisition challenge faced by BFSI and our gross margins on the Zena vertical will become 3X.' Wow!

You may remember that I mentioned in an earlier chapter that I have learnt some vital lessons on leadership in the quotidian-ness of life and parenting. And so it happened that I figured out the trick of great communication smack in the middle of a kids' animated movie!

How this came about was as follows. I have an age-old tradition with my son. We call it 'Back to School' day. The premise is very simple. Throughout his schooling, on one of the final days of his summer vacation, we would carve out a day – me from work and he from his furious cricket playing – and go shopping for all the supplies he would require for the coming school year. We would also indulge in a movie and a meal outside. No matter how big the shoes grew and how advanced the textbooks got, two things remained constant. The movie always had to be an animated one and the meal always at McDonald's.

That particular year, the movie was *Madagascar 2* and my epiphany struck during the denouement when Alex, the lion, and his father are being rescued by their friends who land up in a hastily put together aeroplane. While the brave and motley crew of animals fly the aeroplane, Alex and father hang some thirty feet below in a large iron bucket. Connecting them is a series of monkeys in chain-formation, holding on to each other, not unlike the *Ring a Ring o' Roses* nursery game so popular in our childhood.

Now Alex, being the alpha lion (literally and metaphorically) and finding himself in a particularly sticky situation, attempts to shoot off quick instructions to his friend Marty, the zebra, who is near the flying plane. The only problem is, Marty can't hear him. So Alex needs to rely on the monkeys forming the link to pass the message on. Alex screams to the monkey nearest to him, 'She's got a gun. Let's get out while we can! Pass it on!'

A comical sequence of monkey gruntings ensues, and the message reaches Marty via a very aristocratic British-sounding primate. However, what's happened is a round of Chinese Whispers. 'She's got a gun. Let's get out while we can! Pass it on!' becomes 'Let's have some fun and take out the dam. Basset hound!'

While my son giggled in delight at this sequence, I realised how easy it was for 'let's get out while we can' to become 'take out the dam' in any organisation. After all communication is nothing but a flow of information passed from top to bottom and back again via a chain of primates (ahem), a loop that is repeated for every project, every department and every implementation plan.

Fortunately for Alex and gang, this miscommunication ends serendipitously. The dam gets busted successfully, enemy turns on enemy and mission accomplished, they return home to the adulation of the entire savannah. Now just imagine a communication gap like this between a leader and his team, where one thing is being said but the complete opposite being executed. Would that lead to a happy ending? Absolutely not. Equally imagine when the troops are trying to pass a message up to their leader and the leader is blissfully floating on an aeroplane twenty thousand leagues above sea level and can't or chooses not to hear their desperate pleas.

Miscommunication is an unfortunate by-product of all organisations, big and small. Given the levels of hierarchy that exist between the CEO and the on-ground teams, not to mention the various ways in which an organisation is cut up – regionally, functionally, by cluster – there is ample scope for even the clearest of messages to be distorted. The problem has been compounded today, ironically, by the same technological advancements that are meant to improve connectivity: our wireless networks and multiple screens. As a consequence even people working on the same project no longer sit together, cooped in the same cubicle or lab or around a massive work station, as it happened earlier. They are working out of their homes or from wherever they are holidaying or from another continent in a different time zone, on their laptops plugged in at airport lounges or from cafes. There is limited face-to-face interaction and we all have to rely on hastily typed emails, WhatsApp code language and emojis to convey what we want to say (needless to say, I find that I use the frowny face emoji all the time). And therefore, communicating what needs to be done and the onerous responsibility of making sure that it has been understood by everyone across the width of a far-flung team have become key success factors for the leaders of today.

It has become mission-critical for leaders to be effective transmitters of information and outstanding communicators through simplicity, consistency and clarity of message. While making sure that there is a comprehensive system of reinforcement so that communication across the length and breadth of the organisation is crystal clear and understood by all.

Given the slightest opportunity, people will construe your message in the manner that they deem fit and confidently convey it to others in this new shape and form. This keeps happening until it has gone through so many mental prisms that by the last exchange, you can be sure the message being passed on is almost entirely opposite to the one set in motion! And the organisation has begun pulling in different and conflicting directions rather than towards the single-minded vision you thought you articulated so beautifully in your townhall.

Thus clear and consistent thoughts, simply articulated and repeated ad nauseam, is the only formula of good communication. The best way to do this is to channel that innate nagging mother (or wife or girlfriend). 'Did you get what I just said? Want me to explain it again? Do you require any further clarifications? Are you sure? NOW, TELL ME WHAT YOU UNDERSTOOD!'

And then repeat it all over again!

In our organisation we actually have quizzes after each town hall to make sure that everyone has understood the plan. And they get prizes for getting the answers right too!

That, of course, is not all. Effective messaging is only one half of the communication game. The other aspect, just as critical, is listening. It is something all of us attend to far too little, and the problem is only exacerbated at a more senior level, where instead of listening to what their teams and organisations are saying, leaders become inordinately fond of their own voices. But listening is the bedrock of collaboration and successful team management. Listening to your team, not only with your ears but also with your mind, body and soul, helps you improve your decisions and form the right opinions to drive action.

In one of my earlier organisations, we had a CEO who was a formidable individual. One of the traits that made him so impressive was his uncanny ability to know exactly what was going on in any of our offices, often better than the respective office managers themselves. Such was his knack that we often suspected that he had secret cameras and microphones in various locations. It was only after thirty years that the secret of his success dawned upon me. Today, I can walk into any of our smaller, more far-flung stations and guarantee that I will know the environment of the branch better than the branch manager herself. Does it mean I've put some hi-fi spy surveillance systems there? Certainly not. I might stalk my teams on Facebook on occasion, but even I wouldn't stretch to hidden cameras and microphones! My only secret is that for all my years as a leader, I've been listening with my ears, eyes and mind wide open. Management by walking around and observing what goes on, talking to as many people as possible – in the lift, in the canteen, in corridors – has helped me know exactly what makes our organisation tick (or not). I therefore only require the tiniest exposure to a particular branch before I can correctly gauge the myriad issues that could be plaguing them, what needs to be done next, which initiative to push and which to drop, and how to ensure the branch delivers the desired results.

Nuanced decisions based on factual and timely information gathered from ground zero and unadulterated by false perceptions can avert disasters. Remember the *Titanic*? That is the sheer power of listening. And along with the ability to effectively get one's message across to the team, it forms the crux of being a great communicator, in itself a prerequisite to being a great leader!

IN SHORT

- One of the biggest missteps leaders make is in assuming that they have communicated their expectations just by articulating them at the annual conference.
- Between the talk from the rampart and the walk on the ground, multiple steps need to be taken, including simplifying the communication, keeping the messaging consistent and repeating it as many times as possible.
- Management by listening and walking around is a powerful tool for access to speedy and timely information, often critical in averting disasters.

Prioritising: What Is Your First and Foremost Goal?

Things which matter most must never be at the mercy of things which matter least.

—Johann Wolfgang von Goethe

In the last chapter we discussed how clarity of thought is the first step in successful communication. Only when your mind is clear can you articulate your strategy logically, but ah! There lies the bulk of the problems of our planet, and definitely of the little companies you and I run!

Realistically speaking, the majority of humankind has a very jalebi-fied approach to thinking (jalebi: a circular Indian sweet made up of complex whorls). The root of most problems in organisations, I find, lies in the inability of a leader to be focused and logical in his or her approach and to move from point A to point B in a straight line, rather than by jumping around like a grasshopper. Unfortunately, organisations are stuffed with grasshoppers in more ways than one. This lack of logic results in businesses bouncing about from action to action in a 'one step forward, two steps sideward and one step completely outside the arena' manner, which is highly wasteful and inefficient. Furthermore, the various segments of the organisation are also unable to move together in a concerted and organised manner because there is no clarity about the end goal.

The ability to un-jalebi one's thinking and be absolutely clear on the foremost priority of your business, project, career or next meeting is yet another important component of the journey towards being a great leader.

When I pose the question, 'So, what's your F1?' to any of my employees, I think their minds race immediately towards Formula 1 and whizzing cars, but for me F1 is the very first priority at the top of any list of strategic choices: the non-negotiable goal, your foremost agenda, your North Star. And just like the sailors of yore followed the North Star to get to shore safely, it is the direction set by this F1 priority that one must unflinchingly follow if success as a leader has to be guaranteed.

All of us find ourselves confounded by the immense range of possibilities in front of us at several junctures in our lives – what should we look for in the career we are choosing? Where should we invest our hard-earned money? What should be the focus for this year's organisational strategy – top line, margin or market share – and so on and so forth. We want to have everything, but our limited resources require us to pick and choose between, for example, the size of the apartment, its proximity to work, and good childcare facilities around the property we plan to buy. What should be your F1 when at first glance all three are equally important and desirable?

Unfortunately, another word for focus is sacrifice and human nature is such that we are not able to give something up by making a mindful choice. Consequently, and sometimes injuriously, we end up falling between a stool and a chair in these situations, a place most uncomfortable to our backsides I assure you!

At this stage it is imperative that we select a clear F1 out of the entire range of priorities, ruthlessly and with no qualms at all on having made the choice and sacrificing the rest.

Let me illustrate with an example that will resonate with all of you, dear readers, because this is a type of choice you have struggled with many times in your lives. When studying at the venerable Stella Maris in Chennai, I, like all the girls in the college, was compelled to pick a sport in the spirit of 'healthy bodies make healthy minds', which the dear alma mater propagated to all its disciples. I opted for hockey. Being a quirky mix of hugely unsporty yet highly competitive, my clear F1 for the whole endeavour was to make it to the college team. There was a requirement for a goalkeeper on the team and not very many takers for the same – probably because of how blue it left your ankles with all the hockey sticks you got hit with. (Back then in conservative Chennai, the social repercussions of this were potentially quite grave as it was the only skin that we girls got to display!) I tried for this position and, lo and behold, got picked for the team. What's more, I was fortunate that our college had the best team in the city circuit and our city the same in the state circuit. Since lazy selectors inevitably suffer from the bias of assuming that all players from the best teams must naturally be the best of all available options, before I knew it, I was playing for the Chennai and Tamil Nadu teams as well!

This is not only a brief story of my only claim to sporting success, but also a leadership lesson learnt early in life.

Simultaneously participating in the trials was a dear friend of mine, Leena. You should have seen her. A fine physical specimen she was: fast, lithe and powerful. On top of that, she had outstanding ball control and her stick moved as quick as lightning. If a person were to do a comparative analysis of the two of us, there would be no doubt as to who was more suitable for the hockey team. She however, wanted the glamorous role of the striker of the team. She believed that it was only this position that truly befitted her talent and skill. However, so did many other girls, and competition for the place was extremely stiff. Surely you can guess the moral of the story from here. Yes, she did not get selected for the team. A girl, clearly so capable, did not get into the college team, while another, comparatively much less skilled, not only got into the team but also progressed all the way to the state team. The only difference? The simple matter of priorities.

Now, I may be accused of compromising while Leena who did not make the team would be lauded for not being willing to settle for anything other than what she truly craved. After all, the most stellar heroines remain 'bloodied but unbowed' – there is great cinematic splendour in that. If indeed one has to fail, shouldn't it be in the pursuit of that singular happiness? I don't deny any of this. Neither do I want the generation of today, raised on a diet of self-assurance and intransigence, to compromise their lofty ambitions and not chase their heart's desire. But before you make that judgement and look down your snooty nose at me, the question you need to ask is, what was the first priority or F1 for Leena and me? In both cases the categorical answer was playing for the college team. Seen from that lens, it becomes obvious that she missed out only because she didn't make an informed choice between being on the hockey team at any cost, or playing only if she got the striker role. Either her F1 should have been different or her actions.

That being said, in today's dynamic age, when whole industries can be revolutionised and organisations made redundant in the blink of an eye, one can question whether steadfast adherence to an F1 is good for leaders or not. Doesn't that make them not 'agile', a term considered paramount for organisations to survive today? I would argue otherwise, primarily because prioritising between goals is the domain of strategy and not execution. The latter is performed by multiple teams across organisations and due to the innate entropy of the market, requires flexibility, creative thinking and constant innovation. The former however, is the prerogative of the leadership team and requires focus and a come-what-may rigidity, especially in the short-to-mid-term and especially when everything else is so dynamic. Goals must remain steadfast so that despite the mayhem surrounding them, teams strive towards one end purpose. In heaving seas, if a leader constantly switches between ports of landing, it will inevitably befuddle those under her and the ship will remain at sea forever. Just imagine this scenario: Your CEO communicates that the new focus for the organisation must be bottom-line expansion through cost-cutting measures, even though for the past six months the whole organisation, under the guidance of the same person, had been working towards top-line growth. How will this leave you and the rest of the team? I'm sure you'd be absolutely tearing your hair out. Implementation of any strategy takes time and teams need one vision to follow – to be the most admired delivery firm, to be the best place to work, to have the most radio stations, to have the highest profit margins in the industry. It can be anything, but it cannot be everything. It is the leader's duty to pick this one vision as the F1 of the company or division or team, so that the employees have not only a defined purpose and direction but also clarity in the implementation path.

This very mindful selection of an F1 also helps leaders to remain focused when they are faced with choices during the accomplishment of their promised vision. It can and should act as a sieve through which they can pass all the grandiose ideas they come up with during the course of the year. The failure to ensure this alignment can result in a reality that has nothing to do with the desired vision. Our own prime minister, Mr Narendra Modi, is an important case in this regard. When he ran for office in 2014, his manifesto's vision was 'Sabka Vikas' (Prosperity for Everyone). In which case, the most appropriate F1 would have been economic betterment for everyone, whether rich or poor, in a country that has been struggling to move into a middle-income economy for the past two decades. But the most high-profile initiatives of his reign were demonetisation and GST implementation – the first a scheme to target the country's black money and the second to overhaul India's legacy tax systems. Did either of them have anything to do with improving the universal welfare of India's citizens as the F1? The answer is an unfortunate no. Demonetisation, while penalising black-money hoarders, actually resulted in a hellish period for the vast majority of lower-income individuals, many of them losing their livelihood. No amount of 'shot-in-the-arm for the cashless economy' spin could change that fact.

If he had clearly articulated his F1, demonetisation (democratic in the harm it did to the rich and the poor, the entrepreneurs and the daily wage earners) would certainly not have passed through the sieve.

So to all the current and future leaders reading this book, please do give due consideration to your F1s, not just at the workplace but in all walks of life. You will find it vital in determining the course of action for any major decision you take, and the solid foundation of logic it provides will prove helpful in personal situations as well. So, deciding on a career change or on getting married? What is the absolute non-negotiable you want in the new job? What is that F1 quality your spouse must have? What can be less than ideal?

I find F1 helps bring clarity not just in big decisions but even in small things. On a recent family trip, HD and I were able to wheedle our way out of the general-like manner in which our son was shepherding us from tourist place to tourist place by stressing that the F1 of the holiday was just to spend some relaxed family time together and not to maniacally burn our candles at both ends by hitting each of the items on his list. Given the steadfast preference for logic and structure that he has inherited from us, he had no choice but to agree! See? Having an F1 helps. Just make sure that once you decide what it is, both you and those around you hold on to it like limpets!

IN SHORT

- Targeting multiple goals and priorities is an inevitable part of an annual business strategy, and articulating them logically and clearly is important.
- Even more important is to prioritise between the focus areas. What will be your F1 – the first and foremost goal, the non-negotiable aim for the year?
- As the dynamics of the environment can change mid-course, having decided the F1 early on helps you remain focused should a choice need to be made on a course of action.
- The F1 also helps you make the right call in decision-making processes.

Curiosity Makes the Leader

If you are curious, you'll find the puzzles around you. If you are determined, you will solve them.

—Erno Rubik

Picture the setting of a chocolate company. Alas, it is not the imagination-fueled Willy Wonka factory of our childhood dreams, but just an ordinary Indian FMCG firm. A relatively easy competitive environment and a highly accomplished leadership team have ensured that its brands have become trailblazers in the chocolate market, and indeed are often used as surrogates to define the category. Years of stupendous growth and their stellar market performance have given them a virtually monopolistic market share, but growth has started displaying signs of a slowdown in the past year or so. A new marketing head joins, tasked with rectifying the slump and placing the company back on its yesteryears' growth pedestal.

Into the office he strides. Chest puffed out, self-confident gait. A man who clearly knows what he wants to pull off. Water-cooler gossip starts immediately, a cautious sideways glance is cast. Are changes beckoning? Will there be a rocking of the boat that will throw people over the edge? Or will it just give them a mild queasiness? The eager beaver new brand managers plan to treat this as their opportunity to impress and win brownie points, while the old-schoolers dismiss the rumours, believing past success inoculates them from future pain.

A naturally confident leader he might be (years of witnessing subservience does make people like that, after all!). But there's a reason he is where he is. Behind the air of self-importance that most leaders carry lies a thoughtful and – most importantly – curious nature. Otherwise, this gentleman would not have reached the position he has. And that brings me to my next valuable lesson in leadership – good leaders are naturally curious. They question the status quo and look beneath the hood to see why the engine is working or why it is sputtering. They probe, they question endlessly and they are restless in their quest for more information and knowledge. You cannot be a great leader if your mind has stultified, either because it has become inflexible and refuses to learn new things or because you have decided that as the mistress of all you survey, you already know everything that needs to be known!

Sapiens, the tremendously insightful novel by Yuval Noah Harari, which I'm sure many of you have already read, makes a very relevant point on this front (On a quick personal side note, I take great pride in quoting Harari as I credit myself for having 'discovered' him and his uber-cute Israeli accent in a Coursera course that I had taken long before this book shot him to international stardom!).

In the section of his book where Harari talks about the scientific revolution and how the modern world changed irrevocably after the inventions and innovations of that age, he credits this to a few critical factors, chief among them being the 'willingness to admit ignorance.' Only then, he says, did modern science as we know it truly commence the radical journey of discovery it has been on these past few centuries.

We do not know everything. And more critically, nothing we already know cannot be proven wrong. All concepts, ideas and theories are open to critical challenge; nothing is sacrosanct. And only after having admitted this in the fifteenth century or thereabouts did humans, using their exemplary observation skills, inherent curiosity and the powers of mathematics, go on to build the world as we see it today.

Sadly, as we grow in the corporate world and increase in stature, we forget that what brought us thus far was our spirit of inquiry, our quest for learning, our unquenching thirst to understand and resolve new challenges. Instead, we become prone to thinking of ourselves as omniscient deities and god-like know-it-alls.

'Who can give input to me, a thirty-year industry veteran? I have created this industry let me tell you!'

'Pray tell me what exists that I have not already seen? Malcolm Gladwell said ten thousand hours of practice to attain expertise, yes? Well, I've put in sixty thousand. Now is there anything further you want to say?'

You catch the drift? And if you think I'm exaggerating, trust me, I'm not. All leaders might not act this way, but they very often think like this. As a result, they stop questioning the things around them, stop viewing issues with that critical eye that was earlier held in such regard. But once complacency sets in, the edifice starts to crumble. Even the best product, the best company, the most innovative idea has scope for improvement, but the moment leaders start accepting the status quo, they accept that nothing better is possible. And if you have already reached the peak, the next step after that is only downhill, is it not?

Now let's come back to the story – about the marketing head and the chocolate company. Since I happen to be married to the hero of the story, I am also privy to the next episode and the grand finale in the saga of the search for growth.

The day he walked in, HD decided to shake things up a bit and called for a review of the business without much ado. Now, the organisation was stuffed to the gills with a bunch of old hands who had begun their days as marketing trainees in the same organisation and now roamed its corridors with mighty managerial titles like GM or BM, accompanied by the other markers of corporate VIPism – cabins and personal secretaries. Along with the long association with the company, they had also been hugely successful in the output they had produced for it. So they could be forgiven if they believed that 'they on honeydew hath fed and drunk the milk of paradise', to quote the poem 'Kubla Khan'.

The day of the meeting dawned and the legacy team came in with a swagger and a smile, ready with a ton of data, detailed analysis and complex algorithms to present, prove and rest their case without much ado. They didn't anticipate too many headwinds from the newbie marketing head and the young bunch of new brand managers he had collected around him. Plans for a celebratory lunch, where they would gently indoctrinate the marketing head and his brand team into the easygoing culture of the organisation, had already been fixed for after what they thought would be a breezy exercise in a largely self-congratulatory strategic presentation.

'See, sir? This is the analysis. The chocolate industry is this large; number of premium households into *<educated*

guesstimate of percentage that sounds about right 1> and number of normal households into *<educated guesstimate of percentage that sounds about right 2>* makes the overall market size for chocolates. This is our share over the years, with growth at a stellar rate! It has slowed down in the past couple of years or so, but what can you expect? Just look at our market share! It is 70 per cent! You really can't expect better than that.' They smirked as they lolled about in their seats.

'And why has growth slowed down over the past couple of years or so?' queried HD.

'Sir, what to do? The chocolate market has only grown at this rate. And finally, we have 70 per cent market share, no? It's 70 per cent! A little bit we should also give competition, no?' they said in falsely obsequious tones. Much playful finger shooting ensued followed by a generous amount of back-slapping.

Now any normal manager would have stopped there. He had asked the first layer of questions after all. And things were going fine. Why upset the apple cart? The chocolate market, as the team rightly had pointed out, was after all only so big. There was nothing he needed to do to effect change there. Spun the right way, such an explanation would easily be good enough for most stakeholders involved. And he could get on with the easygoing task of supervising the highly acclaimed team while they continued with their single-digit growth. Only a light touch was required and that would also give him a bit more time for golf.

But then he wouldn't be the hero of this story, would he? His inherently curious nature and desire to get to the bottom of things through a comprehensive interrogation made him probe on.

'And why do you consider yourself a player only in the chocolate market?' he asked in dulcet tones.

The team, while bright, was not necessarily perceptive (and lunch was already beckoning to them spiritually). They continued, at the same time making mental notes that replacing the word 'buddha' with the word 'buddhu' in the song *Main Kya Karun Ram Mujhe*, would generate much laughter at the next office antakshari get together.

'Sir, chocolate company … chocolate market, no?'

'Okay, so tell me this. Where and when are chocolates given and eaten?'

One of the new brand managers piped in excitedly, 'Sir when boyfriend gives girlfriend … err celebrating something … maybe when children pass exams.'

'Excellent!' said HD, glad to see that at least the new team realised what he was driving at. 'And therefore, if chocolate is given during times of celebration, doesn't that mean that we should compare ourselves not just with other chocolate companies, but with whatever is shared during moments of celebration in India, that is, the entire mithai (Indian sweetmeat) market?'

As sure as you have it, when viewed from that lens, the market share of the company in this larger competitive landscape precipitously fell down to sub-1-per-cent levels! Suddenly, instead of facing the difficult prospect of trying to grow beyond 70 per cent, the opportunity in front of the company became a vast untapped mithai market. The growth prospects for a hungry, talented company morphed from a minuscule sliver into a huge and unexpected goldmine.

And it was precisely this approach, built on the foundations of curiosity and a desire to ask questions and know more, that paved the way for the second great wave of this chocolate company's growth, for what I've outlined to you is a very real, albeit simplified case study seen from the front seat in the stalls.

High-quality leaders who continue to break records left, right and centre are the ones who continually ask questions, both of themselves and of those around them. Where are we going? Why are we doing what we are doing? How can this be improved further? Where is the next iceberg going to appear? This is what allows them to constantly push beyond the expected and the obvious, and shatter barriers that box in lesser men and women. Because remember ... curiosity may kill the cat. But it makes the leader!

IN SHORT

- Stagnation of thought is the worst disease a leader can suffer from.
- Constantly questioning the status quo, re-examining accepted practices and revisiting set norms ensures that both people and organisations evolve and grow.
- Why? Why? Why? Three levels of probing are often sufficient to unearth new artefacts of information.
- Learning through curiosity requires daily practice, an openness to accept ignorance and a willingness to change your own mind.

Scylla and Charybdis: You Have No Choice But to Choose!

When faced with two equally tough choices, most people choose the third choice – to not choose at all.

—Jarod Kintz

The aficionados of Greek mythology among you will no doubt know about the tale of Scylla and Charybdis. The Homeric legend goes that these two mythical sea monsters, Scylla manifesting herself as a six-headed sea creature with shark-like teeth and Charybdis as an all-consuming whirlpool, were maritime hazards on the Strait of Messina, located so close to one another that they posed an inevitable threat to passing ships. Veering away from Charybdis meant the risk of being captured and ferociously devoured by one of the monstrous heads of Scylla, while avoiding Scylla meant being stuck in the vortex of doom that was Charybdis. And this tight spot where a tough decision loomed is exactly where our hero Odysseus found himself, midway through his long and arduous journey home to Ithaca after the Trojan wars.

Making difficult choices on a daily basis is an inescapable requisite of leadership (along with the ulcers, and by the way, that's why you get paid so much though no one tells you that at the beginning). When your juniors, your organisation and the people around you are looking to you for guidance, a leader cannot afford to be the metaphorical deer stuck in headlights. You have to decide, take a call and move ahead.

Before I give you my personal take on such decision-making, let's see what our Greek hero, Odysseus, did when faced with the choice he had in front of him. On the one hand, he could steer the ship closer to Scylla, who would ravenously devour six of his best men. On the other hand, he could elect to take on Charybdis, that fearsome swirl of the sea, and risk losing his entire ship and everyone on board. On the one hand, a definite end – an almost willing sacrifice of some of his own crew, men who had loyally accompanied and served him on all his travels. On the other, risking the entire enterprise in an almost calamitous gamble, with only a sliver of hope of getting out of it in one piece. Sounds like a tough decision? You bet it is. But one that a leader often has to make.

I know we all have a rose-tinted impression of Greek heroes – Hercules, son of Zeus, with his God-given daring and strength and Achilles with his (almost complete) invincibility and Trojan-war exploits are only two of the swashbuckling characters that are part of the great legends. Heroes who were the very embodiment of courage, manliness and indomitability, ready and willing to brave any danger or obstacle to save their fellow men or (more often) women! We see them as mythological stars braving the toughest of odds with no more than a second's thought. However, Odysseus was more modern-age CEO than a Greek tragic hero, which is why he, not the other heroes, features in this great saga on leadership! He was shrewd and clever and had in abundance that one element lost on most leaders even today – pragmatism. He knew that if it could be helped, there was no sense in risking the entire ship and bringing an early end to the journey that had cost them so much and was still not over. He went for the well-being of the collective over the individual. Even if Scylla did devour six of his finest, Odysseus trusted the rest of his organisation (here, of course the ship) to survive that loss and for the others to step in and pull their weight accordingly.

I present this decision between Scylla and Charybdis to you today as one of the most important lessons for leaders to learn. One of the toughest jobs of being a leader is having to make constant choices between several equally valid courses of action. Unlike in fiction where everything is black or white, real life operates mostly in shades of grey. Therefore the choices are never between good and bad but mostly between good and better or bad and worse, which is why it's such a harsh task. Did Odysseus not question his own morality for willingly making a judgement that would lead to six of his men perishing in front of his eyes? Did that not trouble him and force him to revisit and question himself endlessly? And what if he had braved the whirlpool and lost? Would he not have castigated himself for the foolishly brazen risk that led to the loss of his entire enterprise (if at all he survived that encounter himself)? Wouldn't he have wished and prayed that when he had the chance, he had been a little more conservative? Or maybe after he passed through Scylla, he would actually conclude that he had miscalculated the odds of losing the entire ship and he should have taken the risk of going through Charybdis instead. The moral and philosophical quandaries are endless.

I'm harping on about this because it is important to stress that leaders invariably have to make decisions in the realm of uncertainty and ambiguity, using limited information. Coupled with that is the fact that in life, no decision is as clear as what good old Karan-Arjun faced – to or not to avenge their innocent father's murder by killing Amrish Puri's most unlikable avatar, spurred on by their overtly virtuous mother across an entire cycle of birth and rebirth.

A few years ago, while at Radio City, I had a top-performing sales manager hand in his resignation letter. Now, he was one of our finest ever sales managers, an individual who had far outstripped his targets year on year on year. And while the rest of the team was also very competent, he stood out as a cut above the rest, so naturally we were very reluctant to lose him. When asked why he was leaving, out came the response that he had received a 20-per-cent increment from elsewhere, which was proving far too tempting to resist. So what would it take for him to stay? Yes, you guessed right. A simple matching of the sums on the table.

You can see the two immensely difficult choices here. As a company, we had a very clear policy that increments would only be given on an annual basis, with no discussions entertained during interim periods. We simply could not afford otherwise. If I stuck to that policy, I risked not only losing one of my key performers but also demotivating his entire team and perpetuating the perception that we were not a company that was willing to pay top dollar for top talent. On the other hand, if I did cave in, what message was I sending? That I was willing to be held to ransom by any individual who felt entitled enough to demand an out-of-turn raise; that I was willing to bend the rules for those select few that I felt deserved it? Was that in any way fair to the rest of the team?

Despite huge pressure from the national sales head who felt his entire world (and target achievement) would collapse if we did not retain this particular manager, in the end, I chose not to give the sales manager the out-of-turn raise. And despite being counselled by HR and listening to their best efforts to retain him, he duly did leave us. The following months were difficult, but other team members stepped in to fill the void, collectively doing this with great enthusiasm and helping us achieve record growth in that station that year. More importantly this particular episode went a long way in reinforcing one of the most important cultural values, that of fairness, which we were trying to institutionalise at that time.

While with the gift of hindsight it's easy to validate the decision made and call it the correct one, should one always take such decisions, where the might of the collective is trusted over the skill of the individual? I'm not so sure. I had taken a risk on the targets and what if they had really not been reached? Would fairness have been seen as a worthy enough payback for non-achievement? I certainly think so, but maybe another leader would have a different point of view. There are no right or wrong answers. There are only choices to be made.

So the key point that I'm making here is that when presented with such choices, leaders in charge have really no choice but to make a decision, no matter how unpopular. However, more often than not, I find leaders are not willing to take a call and just elect to bury their heads in the sand, hoping that the problem will go away. The truth of the matter is that it will not. It will be buried in the subterranean regions of the organisation only to rear its head once more and this time with far more vigour, having fattened itself on the flesh of uncertainty and loose talk in the meanwhile!

Having to make constant choices and decisions on behalf of the organisation and its stakeholders is a recurring theme in a leader's life and we cannot run away from that responsibility. There are several decisions I have taken that have worked out. Equally there are some (only a few!) that haven't, but even those bad choices were better than no choice at all. At least we moved ahead, figured out the mistakes and changed our tactics instead of continuing to dribble near the goalpost and not even take a shot at scoring. Freezing like a deer caught in headlights is the worst thing a leader can do and we should consciously avoid that state of refrigeration.

Many times, taking no decision is far worse than taking the wrong decision, because as we saw with Odysseus, losing six men at least allowed him to continue his decade-long voyage home. Imagine if he had dithered about what to do! Homer would never have been able to get his hero home and the Odyssey, already at a formidable length of twelve thousand and one hundred lines, would have been twice as long!

IN SHORT

- Leaders constantly have to make choices and decisions with limited knowledge of the future and ambiguous fallouts. Only hindsight has a perfect twenty-twenty vision.
- Unlike fiction, choices in real life are never between good and bad, but between good and better, or bad and worse.
- However, making no choice at all will only delay, not delete the problems.
- The faster you resolve issues and move on, the less they will fester in the organisation.

Perseverance

For all things difficult to acquire, the intelligent man
works with perseverance.

—Laozi

Sohan Lal Dwivedi was a brilliant and accomplished poet, a Gandhian and a freedom fighter. A Padma Shri awardee, he is also the author of one of my most beloved poems, *Koshish Karne Waalon Ki Haar Nahi Hoti*. As all good poems do, this one evokes an outburst of passionate feeling in the reader. And since it's about making her feel unconquerable and invincible, it leaves her with an enduring sense that indeed nothing is impossible to achieve in this world as long as one puts in enough effort.

In its spirit, the poem offers one of the most important lessons of leadership I have learnt, and that is perseverance. The poem's prime message is that 'those who try will not fail'. It is as definite as that. Those who try just will not fail. The poet uses two metaphors – one of a little ant trying and ultimately succeeding in her attempts to carry a grain up a wall and the other of a diver's indomitable spirit in repeatedly going to the bottom of the ocean till at last he comes back with a pearl in his hand. This is followed by a beautiful passage on several aspects of perseverance, teachings of timeless wisdom whispered in verse from generation to generation. A message of not giving up. Maintaining positivity in the face of failure. Never running away from the battlefield of hard work. Holding on until you see that inevitable light at the end of the tunnel.

Now, despite all of the poet's (and your elders' – it is after all a favourite parental mantra!) instructions to persevere, you may very well question its legitimacy. And you may be very right in doing so. A long-term relationship that is not going anywhere, a dead-end job, a phase where no one seems to be buying into the great online platform you have launched – all these are unfortunate places to be stuck. Prospects can seem bleak, defeats endless. When should you give up? When should you carry on? Each one of us at some stage of our life has questioned the need to continue with a project or give it up as a lost cause. At these junctures the word 'perseverance' almost sounds like a gimmick, a cliché that is trotted around a little too easily by pseudo-philosophers and pop psychologists.

I understand this viewpoint. Opportunity costs need to be weighed and knowing when to cut the cord is definitely a valuable trait in a leader. However, the world is littered with the carcasses of good ideas, bright initiatives and smart start-up projects, because the people who had created them gave up far too early and far too easily.

When simply as a human being it is so difficult to persevere through periods of hardship and stagnancy, as a leader it is infinitely more difficult to do so. After all, the challenges are all-pervading – an idea ahead of its time, a shrinking market, transitory clients, poor macro-policy decisions or insufficient resources. To add to these, the future is inevitably opaque, with capricious trends, dense and insufficient data and no end of the tunnel in sight! In this complexity, a leader is expected not just to get herself going, but also play cheerleader to the whole team! Does persevering then sound like a gargantuan task? Let's just call that a rhetorical question.

The hard truth however, is that the benefits of having a never-say-die spirit are so visible, the impact so clear, that there is a certain unavoidability in possessing it as a good leadership characteristic whatever the situation, the industry or the environment.

In a nascent industry like radio, for example, volatility in the competitive scenario is par for the course. I have witnessed situations at Radio City where in certain markets we could be doing fantastically, having taken first-mover advantage to establish ourselves as the super dogs for several years, but then the inevitable happens. Competition gets a whiff and moves in to grab a slice of the pie. Before you know it, there are eight other stations vying for the top spot, rates have dropped and the government has decided to come up with another hair-brained scheme a la demonetisation. The sales manager, previously bubblier than an over-the-top Bollywood bahu, now starts coming to work with a hangdog expression. I try to gear him up, get him ready for the fight ahead, but unfortunately what I see in front of me is a broken man, someone who has already given up before the fight. It is after all the far easier alternative; just look at all the unfortunate externalities plaguing the poor soul! Nonetheless, we try to do all we can – we change the product, we bring in new processes, we even change the environment of the office! Doors get moved because vastu decrees it, feng shui means that one wall turns purple, some bells and crystal balls make a surreptitious entry in the reception area. But still no change. It's because the virus has already spread within the entire team. The attitude of their leader, previously so positive but now so despondent, becomes that most unfortunate of self-fulfilling prophecies. He has given up and therefore the team has too.

At this critical juncture, there's only one course left to pursue. It is to remove that leader and bring in someone else who will show that one all-important trait – the will to keep going and not give up. In comes the new person, and with him the original setup of the doors returns, the wall colour changes back to its previous pearly white, and the bells and crystal balls beat a hasty retreat. Slowly, but surely, the numbers become better and the station does return to its former position of glory. It is not a magic elixir. It's not a one week, one month or even a one-quarter fix. It's a dogged and daily struggle that just takes patience and a lot of perseverance from the team.

The underlying theme in the poem is that both the ant and the diver try to achieve their aim multiple times. It's not just a second or even a third attempt. Rather, incessant resolve and tenacity are displayed. In real life unfortunately, all too often, we give up quickly. It could be the fear of judgement or criticism or the fear of time running out or boredom with repetitive tasks or even a slow erosion in belief when, despite best efforts, the results do not come. Especially in start-ups, after the initial series of quick wins that accompany a new launch, there is a period where nothing moves. After the first thousand downloads of the new app, the next thousand take double the time and twice the effort. That is the period when people give up, and that ironically is exactly when there is only one quality that will help you across the valley of death. You guessed it right. It's perseverance!

And if you're still sceptical, still of the belief that perseverance is not a notion worth investing in because it seems that I am just extolling basic, dull hard work, do take a minute more to – yes, persevere. Recently I read a wonderful book called *Thinking, Fast and Slow* by a Nobel Prize-winning psychologist called Daniel Kahneman. The book sheds light on the various ways in which our mind processes and internalises the things around us, from the biases that most of us tend to display to some of the mental shortcuts we inevitably take. While there were many fascinating takeaways for me from the book, there is a key one that I felt was particularly apt to quote here – the concept of regression to the mean.

The concept of regression to the mean is exactly as it sounds. If a person performing a task on a regular basis has a certain competency, on occasion she might perform the task better or worse than that particular level. However, despite these periodic peaks and troughs, her next performance will in all likelihood regress to the mean that is her standard competency. Dr Kahneman uses this concept to beautifully illustrate his research on how we perceive the impact of positive versus negative feedback.

In a study conducted with Israeli fighter pilots, he observes that air force commanders (falsely) believed that their negative comments to pilots for mistakes made during drills resulted in better performances the next time around. On the flip side, they equally falsely believed that the reverse was true. Any praise imparted to the pilots after a good performance resulted in the cocky bastards becoming complacent and as a result putting in a poorer shift the next time around. I know what you're thinking: what brutal hardliners! But I'm sure all of us have had one or two bosses or teachers who behaved quite in the same fashion. Dr Kahneman, though, explains that what the commanders had assumed about how their own feedback worked was in fact merely the pilots' performances regressing to the mean! An incredible learning indeed and it should certainly be quoted to all bosses who are masters of feedback!

But when I contemplate this concept further, I realise this tale is particularly apt for our current topic of perseverance.

My experience, and I'm sure yours as well, is that if you have invested time and effort in building a good team, with a little application, some sincerity and a lot of hard work, most people will do a capable job of any given task. As people go about their quotidian work, they all have ups and downs, victories and defeats, dollops of good and bad luck, the metaphorical drops of rain and pieces of sunshine. The vagaries of life will inevitably mean that there are times when we punch above our weight and others when we are underperformers. But we will inevitably converge to our mean. Because those are the people we really are! In light of that, what conclusions can we draw? That whether we are flying with the wind very much beneath our sails or whether we are walking into a gale, we just need to go on. The mean is inevitable. We will ultimately reach the consistent level of our competencies. And if that bar is reasonably high, the team and we will succeed.

Just like the ant and the diver in the poem, it is grit and determination that will help us reach our goals while lesser mortals are left by the wayside! The woman who wins in the end is not necessarily the most gifted or the most accomplished or the luckiest. She is the one who did not give up.

IN SHORT

- One of the key drivers of success in any venture is the perseverance of the team and its leaders.
- Many difficult situations can be overcome by doggedness and determination.
- A leader's enthusiasm and can-do spirit in and by itself is a powerful motivator and precursor of change.

Planning the Implementation

Strategy is a commodity; execution is an art.

—Peter Drucker

In the last thirty years, CEOs and business heads of various hues, shapes and sizes have meandered across my path and I have had several opportunities to examine them with microscopic precision. Having studied these fascinating creatures at such close quarters and over such an extended period of time, I can confidently tell you that nearly all, or at least 90 per cent of them, get their strategy and vision right; they are highly capable executives and reaching CEO-ship is not exactly a cakewalk after all. But equally most of them fail to execute correctly, so even a well-crafted strategy converts to barely half its potential in reality.

No way! I hear you say disbelievingly. But I maintain the aforesaid as God be my witness!

As I said before, there is no doubt in my mind that most CEOs are fairly good at creating a visionary strategy. They work extremely hard at analysing markets, innovating products, benchmarking the competition and disrupting their consumer touchpoints. All of this is exemplified by the intense brainstorming sessions and passionate debates that are part of the annual off-sites, conducted with great sincerity every year.

But as soon as they come back from these jamborees, the strategy gets locked away in the bottom drawer of the boardroom cupboard, and everyone gets down to the practical business of running the company. As a result, it soon gets forgotten and through the year the business is run around a series of activities and discrete initiatives with tenuous links to the strategy. Even if in the initial enthusiasm, a strategy starts getting converted to implementation in Q1, you can be sure that it gets booted out without a moment's hesitation, either at the first sign of the competition doing something different or at a tiny swing of the market in an unplanned direction!

Factually, most businesses and ideas fail not because there is anything wrong with the idea per se, or that a market opportunity doesn't exist for that business, but because after identifying the opportunity and creating the strategy, entrepreneurs fail to get their implementation right. There is a lovely graph about startups and new businesses floating around in Silicon Valley, which shows that after the initial triumph of launching a new proposition, the idea falls into a deep valley or trough. For an app, getting the next ten thousand downloads after the initial ten thousand is twice as difficult. Selling the next million units after the first million have been sold is more than double the effort. Most entrepreneurs struggle at this phase. If the idea has merit, it will only emerge from this 'valley of death' if the leader gets her implementation right!

I worked with a visionary entrepreneur once who was known for his remarkable capacity to envision what no person had dared imagine earlier. He was considered a pioneer and a revolutionary mogul, but fewer than half of his grand visions converted to reality and those that did mostly failed after a few hundred crores had been spent on them. The reason was simple. He had the incredible knack of coming up with a new dream whilst brushing his teeth every morning, so it was '*Naya din, naya khwab*' every single day for him. To keep up to speed with him, his teams mindlessly spun from executing one idea to another like a posse of demented trapeze artistes, till it made one dizzy just to watch them leaping from rope to rope. No wonder he remains a one-trick pony even to this day.

So why is it that even the creators of the strategy often fail to convert it into action? That's because most managers jump straight from the strategy into its execution. But between the two steps is another vital one, which is planning the implementation, and often business heads miss this crucial step completely!

An architect converts her vision of building an apartment block or an opera house by first drafting its design into a detailed plan, where her CADD drawings include a break-up of the structure and its technical specifications such as materials, dimensions and procedures. Similarly, good leaders first make an implementation road map before hastening to construct their personal edifice.

So what are the critical steps in creating the implementation map of a business?

The starting point of any map, as all of you intrepid travellers or Uber-hailers know, is to begin by pointing the pin at your final destination. And it has to be just a single goal. We discussed earlier the importance of getting the F1 among all the goals of your strategy right. Dozens of strategies I have seen seem to want to do everything all at once: scale up, become profitable, address all segments, have the best distribution network and the highest market share and do this with scarce resources, all within six months. When I ask an entrepreneur what her single-most important and primary goal is, she struggles to give me a one-phrase answer. While I understand that businesses are complex and it is not possible to answer this question succinctly, I also believe that if you cannot articulate the principal business objective in one sentence, you are doomed to non-achievement from the word go. If one part of your organisation is chasing growth, another is chasing margins and yet another is not even sure what you want them to do because of a lack of clarity, nothing will happen, I assure you.

Once you have your F1 in place, you then move to the next step, which is to break up the goal into discrete building blocks. Sometimes looking at a strategy in its entirety is overwhelming for the leadership team. Such a big ask and such little time or so few resources to make it happen. Even for the CEO the complexity is huge. It is horrendously complicated to work across a minimum of seven functions, multiple geographies, different business verticals and then get them to move together in one direction to deliver on a strategy that is constantly being hit by an eight-hundred-pound gorilla of external economic changes, competitive headwinds and the internal dynamics of functions pulling in opposite directions. But it can be done and leaders must not lose heart.

This stage (after taking a deep breath) entails breaking the goals into bite-size and edible pieces. For example, starting with sales targets broken up into tinier sub-divisions by geography, by category, by month. Suddenly instead of that big insurmountable wall, there are smaller fragments that can easily be handled one piece at a time! I remember a large MNC many years ago decided to break the annual targets not into twelve months but equal periods of four weeks each. Suddenly, the sales teams had their yearly target broken into thirteen opportunities, not twelve, and hey presto, the bite became even more swallow-able! So clever, no?

The third step after breaking the objectives into sub-goals is linking the processes, the organisation's development needs and the resources available back to the desired goals.

Now here's the problem – till you figure out not only WHAT to do but also HOW to do it as well, the team will find even the bite-sized pieces difficult to chew. A strategy needs to be converted to process targets as well, which will help achieve those goals. 'Thus I want ten million dollars of revenue, of which three million will come from yield improvement and seven million from more volume of units being sold' or 'If I want to increase the spend per walk-in at my apparel store that sells only jeans, I can do so by adding tops and shirts for which I require to build a competency in my team to understand upper wear, which I will do by ...'

After drafting the design of the building into a detailed drawing of each of the parts of the structure, the good architect then sits down and plans what materials she requires, what type of labour she needs and how she will put the limited budget her client has given her to its best use. Only then does she get down to action lest, after building half a wall, she realises that she has no more bricks left! Thus this third step is extremely critical to match the resources available to the output expected.

Balanced scorecards and 'where to play/how to win' maps that link specific output goals to the specific inputs required are great ways to accomplish the above, and I would encourage all business leaders to learn and use these techniques.

Good managers work hard at thinking about a strategy and then they work even harder at creating an implementation diagram. Only then do they jump (or push their teams) into the fray. An organisation where the leader shows not only what needs to be done but also how to do it, is where intent truly matches action and then magic can be created! To cross the valley of death requires a bridge that is the implementation map, and good leaders definitely need to know how to build it.

IN SHORT

- Most strategies fail because of poor implementation.
- Just as leaders think about strategy in great depth, they need to think about implementation in equal detail before moving into execution.
- Planning and creating an implementation road map is a vital leadership technique, which most managers omit.
- An implementation road map consists of:

  - Clear priorities with the foremost priority (F1) clearly identified;
  - Goals/objectives broken into sub-segments; and
  - Most importantly a plan to link specific input targets, process requirements and resources available, back to the desired goals before setting off on the journey.

Measurement and Monitoring

People don't do what you expect but what you inspect.

—Louis V. Gerstner, Jr.

Running an organisation or managing a team is like being a charioteer. If you are lucky you have a bunch of high-bred stallions pulling your chariot ahead seamlessly and efficiently. As any charioteer would know (and if you don't, please watch *Ben Hur*, and no, *Chariots of Fire* is about athletics, not horse racing!), to make these excellent animals gallop satisfactorily, you need to hold the reins firmly yet lightly in your hands. Too strong a grip and they are likely to lose their enthusiasm and native desire to win and you end up being the one carrying the heavy burden of having to spur them on; too slack your hand on the reins and they are likely to run amuck.

Most managers do not understand this concept at all. And if they do figure out how to achieve this balance at a particular stage in their careers, the moment they get elevated to the next rung of the leadership ladder, they forget it all over again! And gloomily I watch them as they start from scratch yet again, either micro-managing and trying to do everything themselves, or abdicating their responsibilities totally and struggling to figure out the ideal median of delegation that comes right in the centre of the above two.

To be a skilful charioteer, every manager has to accept that in her hands rests the responsibility of winning the race, but equally the realisation that she is not the one running the race – it is her team of charging steeds that has to run swiftly towards the finishing line. And how she holds the reins will determine their success or failure.

So what is the trick in getting this balance right? Over several years of trial and error while working with different types of teams, some majestic chargers, some young ponies and some lame horses, I have figured out that the most important thing is getting the composition of the reins perfect. Once you have the ideal reins in your hand, holding them becomes that much easier and almost instinctive. Thus you don't have to struggle too hard to get the perfect sweet spot that doesn't chafe but gently controls all the same.

I see you look askance at me. Reins, you wonder. Huh? Up until now you thought this was yet another flight of fancy where I was using the analogy of steeds and charioteers as, yes, an analogy. So why am I now suddenly talking of reins not in the proverbial sense but in a tangible leather and weather manner? Hold your horses, dear lady boss, channelise your Fearless Nadia avatar and ride with me on this allegorical journey a wee bit longer.

To me, good quality reins that can help execute a project successfully or run a business well combine two things. The first is high-quality dashboards and regular reviews that have a cadence and momentum and are implemented with military-like rigour. Second and more important is the ability to get the measurement metrics right.

Managers normally understand the review mechanism because reviewing, after all, is their reason for existing and sometimes their only claim to being a leader. If they didn't have a review or two to conduct, what would their life be like? An empty wasteland, a desert with quarterly board meetings as intermittent oases to break the tedium! Many senior and well-respected leaders have made the review processes in their organisation its very *raison d'etre*. So organisations under their charge seemingly exist only for the purpose of being reviewed. One CEO in the media world used to have his reviews from 9 a.m. to 10 p.m. every Monday. For the teams to be ready for this detailed and intense review (every Monday, mind you), they had to start preparing for it the previous Thursday. Which essentially left only two days for the business of the organisation to be conducted. No wonder it was and continues to remain in dire straits!

But while over-indexing the review process, the same leaders don't focus too deeply on what is being measured and what the metrics of evaluation should be. Either they use the wrong parameters of measurement or incorrect data, or they speak in English when measurement should ideally be in Maths only. Doing any or all of the above is getting the entire business of rein-holding utterly wrong and the team is destined only to lose the race.

The erstwhile media CEO I just talked about did incredibly detailed reviews with inordinately poor quality data. So his business heads kept doing very high-level analysis on bad data, leading to the operation of the classic GIGO principle: Garbage In, Garbage Out. Sometimes this practice is not deliberate but becomes a matter of convenience because people analyse whatever is available and in front of their eyes, rather than burrow hard to look for fundamental data that could actually address the issue.

In his remarkable book *How Not to Be Wrong: The Hidden Maths of Everyday Life*, Jordan Ellenberg talks about Abraham Wald, a brilliant statistician working for the Statistical Research Group during the Second World War. The military came to SRG to help them figure out the best place to armour a plane, given that there could only be an optimum level of armouring to prevent the planes from becoming too heavy and hence un-manoeuvrable and fuel-inefficient. Their data showed that the planes that had come back damaged from skirmishes had the maximum number of holes in the fuselage area. This data seemed to suggest that the armour needed to be put in the fuselage. The military thought they had the place and came to Wald to ratify how much armour would be needed.

However, Wald was a genius and the smartest man in the room. He told them that the armour shouldn't go where the holes were, but ought to go where the holes weren't – on the engines. Ellenberg says that Wald's insight was simple. He asked not about the planes that came back, but about those that didn't. The planes that were hit in the engine never came back to base. Thus the engine area required the most armour and not the fuselage, which when hit at least had the capacity to come back to base. The data to look at wasn't that which was available (the planes in front of the analysts' eyes) but that which wasn't (the planes that didn't return). And that piece of information ended up becoming the most important part of the puzzle.

Yet another mistake managers make in measurement is to speak English when they should be speaking Maths. That is, when they should be talking with mathematical precision, they end up waffling in imprecise prose. Jamshed, a very dear friend and incredibly talented management guru, once explained to me how we get our measurements wrong when we do this. The example he used was that of a cook (no more animals lest you think I run a zoo or a farm at work!).

'When we hire a cook,' he elucidated, 'We start by telling him that our expectations are for him to be good at his work. The cook totally agrees and immediately goes about his business of cooking for us every day. Now, as an experienced cook, he understands what it takes to be a good cook; after all he has been working in several houses for so many years. Western, Chinese, Indian, he knows it all and more.' Jamshed smiled benignly while explaining this to me, no doubt carried away by vistas of a delectable buffet. He is a foodie, you see.

'But over a period of time we start getting annoyed with him, although he believes he is doing an exceptional job. This mismatch happens because his interpretation of a "good" cook includes: knowing all varieties of cooking and being a quick worker. Whereas our definition of "good" is using little oil and masala while cooking and coming to work on time and not taking frequent leaves. This discrepancy is because we didn't bother to explain to him what we meant by "good". We assumed it meant the same to him as it did to us.'

Similarly, managers repeatedly make the mistake of not defining the metrics of measurement specifically and particularly, leading to mismanaged expectations and thus wrong actions and disenchantment across the board. Often the pushback I get, especially since I am part of the creative business, is that creativity cannot be measured, that it has to be understood with emotions and a warmly beating heart. This last statement is frequently made by my programming heads, with trembling fingers accusingly pointed at me, the stone-hearted 'suit' with arctic feelings and sub-zero creative sense. Ably rising to the reputation of being emotionless, I retort that everything in the world is measurable and thus monitor-able – love, sex as well as dhoka – and go about proving it to them.

Indeed, among my most notable and successful cases in proving this algorithm true is a performance index score we worked out to measure each song we play on air, based on researching its recall, likeability and fatigue levels. So there!

But the most fundamental error in measurement is getting the metrics wrong themselves. Measuring the wrong things often drives the wrong behaviour and nothing explains this better than the disenchantment economists have recently been feeling over the use of the GDP as a measure of progress. After all, what is the GDP? It is the total value of all goods and services produced in a country and everyone from armchair economists to the most educated businesswoman is obsessed with it, using it as *the* marker of a nation's progress. In turn, all our nation's leaders become solely focused on that figure and orient their behaviour towards improving it the best they can.

But let's dig a bit deeper. Is that something we really want them to do? Will it really improve the health and well-being of our nation's people? The answer is grey at best. GDP does not consider an umpteen number of metrics that we would consider important criteria of well-being – clean air, unpolluted rivers, green spaces, community services, technological progress, stress levels of citizens, the efficiency of public-transport systems, the valuable time a parent spends rearing their child. All these are requirements of the Utopia we want and yet completely ignored in the calculation of the one data point that is supposed to be the single greatest indicator of a nation's progress! It is truly gasp-worthy.

Conversely, let's see all the things that do fit under the purview of GDP measurement – expensive healthcare for chronic diseases; military spend in preparation for war; the lakhs we spend to try and cure our obesity, shoddy stamina or psychiatric issues. Now, are these metrics really what we want our leaders to chase? Of course not. But it's precisely what they will!

I'm not saying that our leaders are cynical enough to wage a war or create societal problems just for political gains like a few basis point increases on the GDP (ahem ahem), but can we really blame them if they do? After all, they are just acting in accordance with what we – the media, the economists and the public – are measuring, and that's the GDP. Behaviour is a direct consequence of measurement and this is just a small glimpse of how actual behaviour can go off tangentially from what we truly want, just because the correct measurement metrics were not selected.

Creating specific, correct and measurable metrics for everything – processes, milestones, targets, the success of a project or a relationship or an organisation and then monitoring them with dedication and a preordained rhythm is the ideal way to hold the reins and drive an organisation to success. Otherwise all we will be left with is heartburn, because we either reached the finishing line too late or actually ran in the wrong race. Or the cook put too much masala in the food!

IN SHORT

- As managers move up the leadership ladder, many of them falter at getting delegation right and fail to achieve the desired balance between micro-management and complete abdication.
- A disciplined cadence of reviews and the right measurement metrics will help them achieve this balance effortlessly.
- To be useful, metrics have to be objective, specific and based on accurate data.
- Often information is not in the data in front of your eyes, but lies below the surface and has to be extracted.
- Everything in life is measurable; we just need to apply mathematical precision and rigour to selecting the right metrics.

Creating Winning Teams

*Talent wins games, but teamwork and intelligence
win championships.*

—Michael Jordan

The first time I became a business head in my career, I had to lead an all-new, all-male team. Naturally I chose to make an impression on my alpha underlings by bringing in an elaborately frosted cake garnished with icing and laden with pink rosebuds for our very first meeting together on a fine Monday morning.

All the Rambos in the room clustered around the table, staring with horror at the cake as if it would detonate any second. A few moments ago these testosterone-infused creatures had been sizing up their opponents and calculating how they would jump over each other's carcasses on their way up the corporate ladder. Now they were internally groaning at the luck of having a female boss who wanted to use them as participants for her kitty party.

I ignored their glowering looks as I brightly urged them to dig into the cake and began to quiz them about their weekend. They were eager to get started on presenting spreadsheets, tallying data and telling me of the revolutionary ideas they had thought of, which would catapult our small company into the big league overnight. But all I wanted to know was how their weekend had gone, what movies they had watched and what fun activities they had done with their friends and families.

With immense reluctance and much foot-dragging I was allowed a peek into the human beings that lay behind the sharp suits and hungry ambitions that populated the room.

Obviously it was not just friendly conversations and small talk and we did get to work eventually, much to the men's relief. But every Monday morning, without fail, there would be a cheerful fruity and flowery cake waiting at the table, signalling both the start of a hard working week and inviting a freewheeling chat to begin it with.

It took many weeks and awkward silences for my macho heroes to reveal their inner softies, but it did happen. The men in the room on that first Monday only saw strangers and competitors when they looked at each other. But over a period of time they started seeing each other as friends, confidants and teammates. The cake went from being an object of scorn to a symbol of community, friendship and togetherness.

Maya Angelou said, 'I've learned that people will forget what you said, people will forget what you did, but people will never forget how you made them feel.'

In the past three decades, many of the teams I've led have disbanded or evolved and changed. Yet my cake meetings have become the subject of folklore – filled with the nostalgia of memories of working together, some of the victories we achieved, the failures we encountered and the joys and conflicts we shared that powered us through both good and bad times.

Good teams do not happen by chance. It takes immense effort, patience and diplomacy to turn a group of individual stars into a bright galaxy. If done right, a collaborative team will not only light up the department and the organisation to which it belongs, but it will also enrich the lives of the people in it immeasurably.

But when done wrong, it backfires into a cascade of supernova that has far-reaching destructive consequences. Instead of uniting kindred spirits and encouraging comradeship, it festers jealousy, ego and single-minded goals of self-interest. And the leader spends more time managing internal conflicts than trying to fight the enemy outside. In my experiences as a leader, there are mistakes I've made and learnt from, those I've witnessed and sworn to avoid and those I am in the process of making. Here are three key lessons about good team-building that this journey has taught me.

The first and foremost rule in the team-building gamebook is to create trust among team members. Competent leaders work hard at securing extraordinary individuals for each of the functions their team must perform. But they stop there. They think that they've got great people in the finance, HR, marketing and supply-chain roles. They give directions to each of them, forgetting that there is an interplay that has to happen between them, which requires each player to have faith in the other.

A team isn't created automatically just because people work together in a shared environment. The belief that there is an auto-pilot that starts operating when you've got the right people in place is misguided. A manager needs to spend an inordinate amount of time ensuring that teammates interact with each other well. And trust is the foundation that builds a successful professional relationship.

Unfortunately, there's no medicine you can hand out with the guarantee that on popping the pills for seven days, trust will build. It takes time, something that as a leader under immense pressure to deliver, you might not have.

But you can fast track the process by getting your crew to spend time with each other. That's how individuals start recognising fellow teammates as human beings with strengths and weaknesses instead of automatons with whom they share breathing space. Understanding allows for connection and bonding, which then leads to trust.

A majority of leaders miss this non-negotiable aspect of team-building. The few who do understand it uphold it extraordinarily well. When they sit and discuss strategy and plans of action, when they do weekly dashboards, when they take people off-site for meetings, when they call them home for dinner and yes, when they serve them cake week after week – they force togetherness, a precursor to building trust.

The second and extremely powerful mechanism for building teams is to bind them together around a common goal or purpose. Clever leaders use different ploys to make that happen, including sometimes using a mutual enemy to achieve this aim. For all of those who have seen the movie *Chak De India*, there's a scene that aptly exemplifies this manoeuvre.

The ragtag group of awkwardly assembled hockey players are sitting at a restaurant despairing about their future because they are about to be disbanded. One of the reasons is that they have not been able to convert themselves into a synchronised team. At that moment a group of ruffians enters and begins harassing the Manipuri girls in the group. Immediately the women spring into action and take on the harassers with immense bravado and gusto. As satisfying as it is to watch them beat the ruffians into pulp, it's even more fulfilling to see how a team gets galvanised together when they identify a common target. That's the moment in the movie when things turn around for the hockey team and that's exactly how it happens in real life too!

Success in the business world depends on collaboration and teamwork and not the individual performance of the superstars, valuable as they may be. This brings us to the third lesson – you have to certainly make the members of your team feel special, but you have to do this while enforcing the belief that they're good not in isolation but only in the context of the team.

We may be lured to the halls by a Shah Rukh Khan or a Madhuri Dixit. But it's the behind the scenes team of director, producer, writer, cinematographer and so on who make the movie what it is. Not just the star who comes on screen in all her or his cinemascopic glory, reciting dialogue to much acclaim. As a society, however much we cherish the stories of lone rangers and all-powerful heroes who will save the day single-handedly with six guns blazing all at once (and are conditioned to emulate such narratives ourselves), in real life, good work is always powered by team effort. In the initial days of the radio renaissance in India, when competition suddenly burst onto the scene, we lost a couple of our prized RJs to new rivals in the market. One of them replicated the exact show he used to do for us on his new employer's channel. But it fell flat and that's when it dawned on him, and the rest of us, that while he may have been the star of the show, he didn't make the show what it was. It was a team of producers, music managers, sound engineers and the programming head who were together responsible for the magic.

As all of you, dear readers and leaders of tomorrow, climb the career ladder, I notice that women do a far better job than men in leading teams. That's because of the intricate ways women – irrespective of class, caste and privilege – need to navigate the world and relationships around them. This gives them a masterclass in dealing with the mercurial moods and assorted needs of team members. For example, women ace at conflict resolution, because that's what they have been doing all their lives.

Professional success inaccurately leads to an inflation of the ego, but women are thankfully insured against this particular trait. Men, who don't need to learn to see the world from any point of view other than their own in order to survive, have a narrower lens that tends to get more dictatorial as they ascend the hierarchy. He is the general. The employees are his troops. That's a good enough foundation to build a team. Most male leaders I've witnessed are comfortable with the notion that the common purpose to which the team members need to pledge their loyalty is them. That 'love me, admire me, adore me, follow me' is a good enough call to arms.

Women trained from birth to see everything from the world's gaze (sometimes at the cost of their own viewpoint) will actually put in the effort to collaborate, to develop the strengths of the team, to cajole and massage egos, to educate them and to scold them when necessary. It is true that there are plenty of bad women team leaders and extraordinarily good male team heads. But the rigorous social conditioning that both men and women are subject to from childhood makes such cases the exception rather than the rule.

The workplace is an infinitely better place when we are surrounded by friends we like, role models we admire and subordinates we enjoy mentoring. Given that we spend the majority of our lives at work, being in charge of a group of people is not a responsibility we should take lightly. Getting to build and maintain a great team filled with trust, bonhomie and camaraderie, a team that plays together in complete synchronisation with each other is one of the greatest privileges of that position and imperative to achieving victory. Ask any great sports coach or otherwise learn from Shah Rukh Khan as he takes his gaggle of women hockey players to victory in *Chak De*!

IN SHORT

- Building winning teams is a precursor to success as a leader.
- Just hiring talented individuals and getting them together is not team-building.
- It requires creating trust among them, bonding them to a common purpose and then enforcing within them a code that says that the team is larger than any individual supernova.

Kehna Karna Nibhana: Consistent Commitment

Your consistency says a lot about your commitment.

—Rasheed Ogunlaru

'Didi!' my cousin chirps on the telephone.

'Yes, Anjali? How can I help you?' I respond, using my cold and stoic 'official' tone, hoping that it will ward her off a little quicker. I have been practising this technique with limited success on family members who call unexpectedly in the middle of a weekday, not because there is anything wanting in my stoicism or coldness but because most of them have become inured to my inherent grumpiness.

She continues, undeterred (I told you so). 'I'm in Delhi, Didi! For my neighbour Abha's niece's wedding. You remember her, don't you? Beautiful girl, you would've met her at my fiftieth birthday party. She's getting married to this rich Delhi guy, son of an industrialist of course, and I'm here for the wedding ... fancy it is, let me tell you that, people are dressed to the heights, but I'll match them bling for bling, after all I have that solitaire necklace that we bought with aunty-ji last year ... and remember that pink saree I had shown you that I was wearing for the wedding? Well, I changed that, because Abha's mother gave me such a pretty one, Sabyasachi's new collection that too ... said I reminded her exactly of herself when she was younger. Well, herself or her sister, I can't remember but she said one of the two definitely, and now ...'

Given that it's a Wednesday afternoon and I'm currently in the middle of a series of office crises, I try to usher her closer to the point.

'That's fascinating, sweetie. I'm so happy for you. But why have you called?'

'Oh, yes, yes, yes, of course. Well Didi, you remember that saree material you had liked so much when we went shopping last time? I found exactly the same one at this awesome little store here, even better quality if that's possible, just fabulous that material, feels so nice in your hand I can't even tell you. I also spoke to the store owner and he promised to give me a discount, at a friends-and-family level you know. And I thought to myself that I just have to buy it for you Didi, I just have to. It'll after all go so well with your whole look, good for office and after work as well. I know for a fact that you'll look very nice in it, so what say, tell me no, shall I?'

Awash like the Liril girl (people, especially males of my generation, may remember her) under this verbal onslaught, I paused for a moment of reflection. Now, my cousin is many things. As a trained socialite and shopaholic very much in the know, she is on intimate terms with every vendor from Crawford Market to the upper echelons of high-street fashion and has the uncanny knack to gauge the most excellent deals. Unfortunately, an abider of commitments she is not.

Nonetheless, unfailingly polite as always (and in a hurry to end the conversation), I tell her that bringing me the saree would be extremely nice of her and that I would greatly appreciate it if she did that, given of course that it didn't inconvenience her too much. I agree despite knowing precisely how the story will play out. Sure enough, as predicted, despite her initial enthusiasm Anjali fails to follow through with her commitment of getting me the saree.

At this juncture, let me introduce you to three words that I hold very dear, the ones that will form the bedrock of this chapter's leadership lesson. They are 'Kehna, Karna, Nibhana.' Allow me to define them for you very briefly below:

Kehna – To say

Karna – To do

Nibhana – To do always. Unfailingly and without question.

Unfortunately, there is no way to translate Kehna, Karna, Nibhana (KKN for future reference) into English without losing its essence. The term it would come closest to is 'consistent commitment'. In our busy worlds, where all of us look to become self-actualised souls at the earliest age possible, we tend to cram as much as possible into our daily lives. We want to work hard so we may be professionally successful and earn a lot of money, but we also want to help our ailing parents, dote on our children, tend to our gardens, gossip with our friends and indulge in the adolescent fantasies that all of us are still waiting to achieve – whether that is learning French or becoming professional musicians. And despite knowing somewhere in the deeper recesses of our mind that all is not achievable, we plunge on unabashedly and a tad arrogantly. As a consequence of this, apart from inevitable burnout, we leave behind a wasteland littered with broken and unfulfilled promises – to friends, to family, to colleagues and to ourselves.

This is where the philosophy of KKN supersedes the concept of a mere promise. Because the value system that is at the heart of KKN is one of careful and mindful thought. KKN says that whatever I commit to do, I will deliver. And I will deliver consistently and repeatedly. KKN can therefore never be a litany of half-hearted, casual promises. Rather, it has to be those carefully deliberated oaths you have made to yourself and to everyone around you, because you know you have to fulfil them each time and always. Constantly and consistently. To the best of your abilities. As a result you make sure that you don't make these promises either lightly or loosely because you have to keep them not just once or twice, but upon every given moment of asking.

Now, when Anjali promised to bring me that saree, it would quite possibly have been one of the several casual promises she made to various people over the course of that one day. Due to their inherently trivial nature, the fulfilment or non-fulfilment of these promises would have mattered very little to her. She would do (or not do) whatever happened to convenience her at that given time. As a result, she treated this 'promise' not as something that was second nature to her, a commitment she had to fulfil, but as a mere triviality that dissipated with the same bubbly enthusiasm with which it had arisen.

Now let us examine the alternative. The one that KKN extolls. As I've said before, it is about careful thought. Promises that you hold as an extension of the self, and therefore want to complete both now and in all the instances to come. KKN manifests itself in behaviour that others see as always holding true and steadfast, no matter what the circumstances. Regular readers of my blog will recall our family dog, Scamper, as being a steady source of inspiration in the way he lived his life. And here, he serves as one as well. From the day he entered our house to the day he unfortunately passed away, it was almost that he had made it his daily duty to bring as much happiness as he could to those around him – from my husband and I, to my son and mother, and even to our household help. Whoever needed a leg up, he was there to provide it with a lick, a nudging paw or a look of love in his large, innocent eyes. No matter what the circumstances were in his life, this commitment was second nature to him. And it was unfailingly adhered to whether he was happy or sad, healthy or ill, hungry or full-bellied. That is the very essence of KKN.

When KKN is done just for yourself, it makes you a powerful individual, one who has a very clear set of values and stands by them and can be relied upon as a trustworthy person who fulfils all her commitments. And that's a great thing – something for all of us to aspire towards. But when this attitude of KKN is extended to a whole organisation – that's where the magic really happens. Because at that level, it can lead to the construction of a powerful organisational culture. When an organisation promises something and then consistently delivers on that promise, it builds a culture of reliability and trust among all its stakeholders. And those are important adjectives for any business, in any industry. Trust and reliability.

Now, this doesn't happen easily. KKN is a challenging concept to understand and imbibe. I have worked tremendously hard to get this point across to my organisation and especially the ones in charge of helping establish the culture – the HR team. While today I can say that they have indeed passed with flying colours, the path hasn't been one devoid of roadblocks. HR professionals, even the best of them, are notoriously excitable. While well-intentioned, they often want to run a range of interventions without ever thinking them through entirely. And nothing excites them more than creating new policies for a company. It is with this enthusiasm that one day a senior HR professional at one of the businesses I manage came up to me.

'Ma'am! The team and I have been thinking a lot about the things that we can do to make our 'Great Place To Work' ranking even better next year. One of the things that we've thought about, and ratified through the employee survey, is that an open-plan policy where everyone is sitting together really makes employees believe that all of us are equal. It encourages bonding and transparency too. You always say, if we believe in something, we should really come out and champion it. Well, we believe in this. And we'll walk the talk too. During your town hall, we will announce that we are breaking down all the cabins and all of us will sit together and you will sit right in the centre ...'

While she proceeded to list various activities intended to dismantle any real or imagined barriers between all one thousand employees, I was horror-struck and could only visualise a disastrous fishmarket kind of open area, with me sitting enthroned in the centre like some deity and everyone shouting hysterically around me (our organisation is slightly loud, by the way). I decided I had to nip the idea in the bud immediately, and it's not because I doubted that her research was correct. What she hadn't thought through was the fact that nothing irritates employees more or makes them quite as disillusioned as empty promises made by their company and especially their seniors. If a company professes that it'll drive transparency through openness for everyone, employees expect that it will jolly well do that for all concerned, without exception. That is precisely also the sentiment of KKN, which was a key value system at our organisation.

When it came to this situation, no matter which way I examined it, an open-plan office was not something we could adopt. Apart from the practicality, there was also the issue of private meetings and confidential discussions. I remembered visiting a client's office early in my career where I found the CEO, after launching a massive search operation, sitting behind three metres deep foliage resembling a verdant rain forest. When I enquired about his love for greenery, which seemed a bit excessive, he sheepishly told me that it was his way of getting around the open-plan policy his US headquarters had ordained be followed in all offices! I asked my HR head whether she was willing to hold her meetings in front of everyone and conduct hiring and firing discussions in an area resembling a fish-bowl. Now, given that HR teams think of recruitment as their particular domain secret and the holy grail that has to be kept hidden in a deep, dark vault twenty thousand leagues under the ocean, I had obviously touched a nerve and immediately she quailed at the thought, saying that for certain things we would obviously have to have cabins and private rooms. And that was where the philosophy of KKN broke down. Consistently doing what we said also meant doing it across the board for everyone, with no exceptions.

KKN is a very valuable lesson for all of us in life, as individuals, as managers, as family members and as leaders. If you commit to something, please honour the commitment however trivial it is – like reaching a meeting at a designated time or returning that phone call. And if you say you believe in punctuality, then please be punctual, unfailingly and without question. Kehna, Karna, Nibhana. And if you can't, don't bother making that initial promise. That's okay. No one will think any less of you.

As a leader, if you can create a culture that values KKN, I promise you, the organisation will run almost on its own, like a well-oiled machine with everyone delivering whatever they committed to. What more can a leader want?

Now let's just hope I get my saree someday.

IN SHORT

- Beyond walking the talk is another realm of leadership that says it's not just about walking the talk once in a while, but walking it always. Once you commit to something you must fulfil your promise always and consistently.
- Steadfastness in honouring the commitments you make, whether big or small, demonstrates your reliability as a leader.
- Exceptions and ad-hocism are the biggest reasons for mistrust in an organisation and are value-eroders of a culture.
- An organisation built on the principles of consistently delivering on its commitments can build trust and create immense value among all its stakeholders.

Culture Vulture

The culture of a workplace – an organisation's values, norms and practices – has a huge impact on our happiness and success.

—Adam Grant

'Sports is life in quick motion,' HD proclaimed, looking down his imperious nose at me as he sizzled with righteous wrath and indignation at a comment I'd just made. It so happened that the entire extended family had gathered around some cricket match on TV and they were exhibiting assorted levels of heartburn, starting with resentment and moving right up to red hot rage at an umpire's faulty decision. Amid this maelstrom of masculine feeling I had innocently (and rather charmingly, I thought) observed that most of the pot-bellied men who lost their minds at every sporting event on TV had themselves not entered a gym or engaged in any sporting activity in decades. So their devotion to this athleticism surprised and puzzled me with its intensity.

In a salutary tone that was meant to correct my profound ignorance and to protect his brethren from unfair criticism, HD launched into an impassioned speech: 'All the highs and lows of life – the travails, the failures, the success – happen in a one-day match or a ninety-minute game. Whatever takes place in the compressed duration of a game plays out in a longer format in real life too.' He continued reverentially, 'Because ultimately sport is a metaphor for life itself. That's why we connect with it so intensely!'

I normally pay very little attention to the lectures HD is prone to giving me every once in a while (Reminder on why this is so in chapters thirteen and fourteen on menopause and mid-life crisis.). But the fact that sport and life have a lot in common with each other resonated deeply with me, because there is certainly one portion at work where I have definitely applied lessons from sport, and that's in the process of organisational culture-building.

Arsenal fans the world over, whether in Delhi or Dubai or a pub in London, belong to one tribe, just as HD and assorted Mumbai Indians cricket fans across the globe belong to another. They are bound by fervent loyalty to the teams and to the players and fused to each other by an unimpeachable sense of brotherhood. Loyalty to a team or to a sport fuels a sense of belonging, which in turn gives rise to a strong sense of identity based on a shared set of values. This invisible sentiment of togetherness is the secret behind the legions of followers great sports teams build up. It is also the secret sauce that helps certain organisations manage to repeatedly attract and retain talented employees. Intelligent and far-sighted leaders recognise the importance of creating this spirit of belonging, which is why they work as hard at building the culture of the organisation as they do at crafting its strategy.

In the decades gone past however, workplace culture-building was never considered macho enough to be taken seriously. It was assumed that culture, with its touchy-feely connotations of warmth and bonhomie, had tenuous links to organisational performance and was thus unimportant.

CEOs were quick to talk about strategy, budget, profit, revenue targets. These muscular centres of success were accorded a prominent seat at the boardroom table while ethos and culture, in all their intangibility, remained shrinking violets in the work environment.

Of course the consequence of this was not that an organisational culture did not get built at all. It did, but surreptitiously and informally.

The truth is that if leaders don't build culture mindfully, it gets built based on the random behaviour of a few senior people. Since no standard expectations of behaviour have been set for team leaders, they behave as they deem fit. And the culture that emerges out of this equation becomes a hodgepodge of senior leadership styles till one fine day you wake up and realise that inadvertently, your organisation is now known for petty politics or average performance standards or sluggishness.

When we recruit people, we do so for their functional skills. We don't tell them the behavioural expectations the organisation has from them. We only tell them our expectations in terms of their performance. But there is also an attitudinal aspect we need to focus on if we want to ensure the creation of a well-thought-through culture. When we clearly define what we want to stand for – be it fairness, respect for individuals, prioritising teamwork, etc. – we also by default demarcate what we are not. Believing that culture can drive business results and then thoughtfully creating it based on the organisation's business exigencies is a critical first step in organisational building.

I strongly believe that the success of Radio City as a leader in its industry is primarily because of the culture we worked very hard to build in a purposeful and careful manner. Many years ago when we first started working on Radio City's go-to-market strategy, we realised that we would be competing with the big daddies of the radio industry. Be it Times of India or Sun TV, every major media house had a radio network. We were owned by an emerging private equity fund, an ownership structure that had a default perception of being cutthroat and short-term oriented. So why would people come and work for us?

Very early on we decided that it was our culture that was going to draw top talent to us. Today we are one of the leading radio networks in the country and among the top ten places to work not only in India but also in Asia. We competed against giants and won. From a small four-city boutique network, we grew to one of the largest and most profitable radio networks in the country, en-route going through an ownership change, one public market listing and headwinds that buffeted us so often that turbulence management became our default style. The only thing that kept us on course was the lodestar of our culture. We did many things based on it and refused to behave antithetical to our values. Over a period of time this consistency created a strong and palpable culture that ensured that many of the best people in the radio industry continued to be Radio-Cityzens in good times and in bad. Culture may be an invisible differentiator but when done right, it can become a massive deliverer of profit. And Radio City is a textbook example of this.

Fortunately, now there is empirical evidence that there is a direct link between culture and performance and results. As India's economy increasingly becomes services-centric, for many organisations the product they sell is their employees and the behaviour of these employees. What an

RJ says on-air or what song a music manager decides to play defines a radio station's product. Similarly, in a bank, how a teller behaves with you and how smoothly a bank manager resolves your problem – these are the products customers are dealing with. How well the Swiggy guy delivers your food and how hospitable the employees of a hotel or restaurant are, define the organisations' brand and are centred around human connection and interaction. And therefore, the company's culture directly influences not only its employees but also the product's perception in the market and thereby its results.

So apart from doing it mindfully, what else does it take to build a good culture? We have an unbelievably successful model to take pointers from when it comes to setting up culture at our workplace – religion. Be it the major faiths of the world or the little-known sects that command small but fanatical followings, religion has fine-tuned the art of using culture as a powerful binder to build communities and forge connections, establish moral codes of behaviour and offer sources of faith and support that are intimately personal and universal at the same time.

Religious cultures are created using rituals that people are supposed to follow, value systems they need to adopt and codes they need to adhere to. They are then propagated across the globe using stories that are told across generations.

In the recession of 2008-09, all our competitors had to resort to dismissing people in order to survive. We didn't do that. Instead, company seniors decided to take a pay cut in order to ensure that in tough times, none of our employees and teammates lost their jobs. The recession is now a decade old. It is history. Organisations and the world have moved beyond those dark days. But I make sure that this is a story that gets repeated and retold at every possible occasion. Lest people forget. Because this is a story that defines our empathetic culture.

What are the defining legends of your organisation, the ones that will galvanise employees into action?

Apart from mythology and storytelling, meaningful rituals are at the heart of a religion's pull for its followers. At Radio City, rewards and recognition have been an important aspect of creating pride among employees about the work they do. Over the years, many rituals have been created around this aspect, such as 'Cheers to Peers', a monthly gathering where people come together to thank someone publicly for some help they have been given or 'Ring A Loud', a ritual where, if a person believes that she has done something extraordinary, she comes and rings a bell to tell her colleagues about her achievement. Some years back, I had initiated a small ritual when someone moved into a cabin after a promotion – a sure sign that she'd moved up in life. I would give them a Bourneville chocolate. The chocolate was chosen for its occasion appropriate tagline: 'You don't buy a Bourneville. You earn it.'

When I moved to an expanded role in the organisation where Radio City was not under my direct purview, I stopped performing what I thought was an inconsequential ceremony but the employees did not forget it. A few months passed and then the HR team told me, 'Ma'am, the new GMs who have been promoted and have moved into cabins are feeling very bad because you have stopped giving the chocolates.' So, I sheepishly restarted the ritual.

In the larger scheme of things, giving a bar of chocolate may seem like a trifling gesture to an outsider. But it had become part of the folklore at Radio City and an important moment in our employees' career journey.

Employees are constantly on the lookout for a culture that calls to their sense of purpose and value systems. Many founders at startups today believe that they can capitalise on this zeitgeist through token actions. A newbie boss thinks, 'Oh, I've built a great culture because I've put a green couch in the storeroom for people to sleep on. Or because I've put a foosball table in the common room or because everyone can wear whatever they want to work.' And then wonders why he has such high attrition levels despite the free ice-cream.

The difference between token simulators of culture and the real thing is when a leader's actions in culture-building are based on authentic values that she truly believes in.

The 2016 animated Disney film *Coco* enchantingly explores the arc of little Miguel growing from a self-interested individual to a key player in his family's rituals. The Dia de Muertos or the Day of the Dead celebrations hold no meaning for Miguel until he travels to the land of the dead and understands the full import of the festival. He realises that our dear departed remain alive in another world because we remember them as part of the rituals during Dia de Muertos. They truly die only when they start being erased from our memory and we stop remembering them. So to keep them alive in the other world, we celebrate Dia De Muertos and that is the true import of the ritual.

Good cultures are built not on hollow rituals but on rites attached with deep significance. The chocolate that we give our new GMs is not an empty celebration; behind that lies a statement that says, you have earned it. It is a recognition that the person truly deserves to be where she is and she has worked hard to get there. Equally it conveys to all that unlike in other organisations, promotions at Radio

City are not a natural outcome of tenure alone. You have to work hard to get a cabin!

Such a small ritual, but such deep meaning – motivation, recognition and a meritocratic culture. The Bourneville conveys all of that and more.

People crave to be part of something bigger than themselves. If a good culture at the workplace can tap into that innate need, then you've got the road map to harness potential into productivity.

Philip Kotler once said, 'Culture eats strategy for breakfast,' and I think that is the most relevant advice the sage has ever given us to manage our businesses and create strong and sustainable organisations.

IN SHORT

- Culture is a critical, albeit invisible, differentiator of success and sustainability in an organisation, because it has the power to unite people around it.
- Leaders need to work purposefully towards creating an engaging culture lest it build unconsciously around undesirable values.
- Strongly upheld and practised values, storytelling and meaningful rituals are some powerful tools to build great organisational cultures.

Personal Accountability:
I Am Because of Me

Whether you think you can or you think you can't, you're right!

—Henry Ford

As we bring our conversation on leadership to a close with this final chapter, my dear readers, in the spirit of the lessons we learnt about good communication, I would like us to take a few moments to reflect on the crucial and I hope implementable suggestions that have been made in this section of the book.

When we began our journey of understanding the art of leadership viewed from the battlefield, so to speak, we saw how much we could adapt from a role that many of us have already been playing for several years now, that of child rearers. As parents, we dole out discipline and love in equal measure to help our children become better individuals and while doing so we also teach them to deal with the big, bad world with courage and fortitude. These are valuable leadership lessons to manage teams too. We learnt of the power that comes with listening to those around us and how implementation can be facilitated and goals achieved by a truly clear mind that has its priorities set correctly. We discussed the importance of being curious and asking questions, of making hard choices and of persevering through the trying times that all of us have faced at some point or the other in our lives. We made note of some of the common biases that leaders fall for – a pro-strategy bias and a negative skew against implementation, and the dangers of subjective measurement metrics. Lastly, we spoke of clearly defining and sustaining values, promoting genuine trust among teams, unfailingly keeping commitments and using all these as building blocks to create empowering and engaging cultures.

Each of these lessons has helped me be better at my job, and I hope they will one day do the same for you. I am sure that all lady bosses, and even some of the gentlemen bosses out there, will be able to incorporate the lessons learnt here and use them for both personal and professional growth. But ultimately, all these suggestions and any additional advice that other leadership gurus might advocate become irrelevant if the one trait that binds them all is missing. And that king among kings, Shahenshah-e-Alam of all leadership traits is personal accountability.

It is the single-most important driver of leadership in my opinion. I say this loudly and vociferously because I have seen too many talented managers unable to evolve to great leaders only because this particular characteristic was missing in their make-up.

When a very young child loses her ball while playing, she comes to her mother and happily says, 'Mama, the ball is lost.' Note the use of words. The child believes that the ball lost itself all on its own. And consequently it doesn't upset her. She believes her mother will take care of the situation and indeed the doting parent rushes out to the play area, scrambling around for the lost ball, frantically calling husband/assistant/parents/employees to tell them to drop everything and look for a replacement. However, when this same child grows up a little bit and loses the same ball, she returns crying, 'Mama, I lost the ball.' It's a complete turnaround of both syntax and associated emotion. This time, not only does the child feel terrible about losing the ball, but also for the first time in her life admits that it was her fault that the ball got lost. Several studies on developmental psychology indicate that this is the point in the child's growth (usually around the age of six) when the transition to adulthood truly begins. Because that's the behaviour that adults are expected to demonstrate, to take responsibility for their actions and the consequences thereof! To whit – personal accountability. 'I lost the ball.' The ball didn't lose itself of its own volition. Neither did some malignant universal force direct its disappearance. It was me and only me.

The reason I am highlighting this issue of accountability so vigorously is that most people struggle to accept onus, especially in negative situations. Despite being grown-ups, they morph back into that preschooler who happily says the ball disappeared through no fault of hers. This fundamental attribution error makes us prone to patting ourselves on our backs when things go right (and men are a little more inclined to doing this than women are), but also just as swiftly blaming the external situation around us when things go wrong. Sales targets not met? Must be the bad economic conditions. Marriage failing? It was because our kundalis didn't match. Child turning out to be a brat? Surely it's all the company he's been keeping at school. And before we know it, we start blaming everything but ourselves for the shortcomings and disappointments that our lives are inevitably littered with. For it is the easier route to take and so much better at ensuring a good night's rest and certainly far more preferable than seeing our own errors reflected in the mirror of our benighted circumstances.

My friend, Saumya, one of India's supremely talented women CEOs, quotes an example here of how one of her childhood friends, Vibha, insists on launching into a tirade every time they meet, of how she was in fact the better student during their school days, the one who always came first in class and was told by all and sundry that she was destined for great things in life. Unfortunately, she was stifled by her mother-in-law who wanted her to have babies as soon as she got married, which is why she did not scale the heights expected of her when compared with Saumya. Vibha also makes pointed references to all the strokes of luck that she believes fell Saumya's way, which according to her is the only reason why Saumya became a leading light in the industry while Vibha was left an unhappy victim of circumstances.

If only one day someone would recite to Vibha that famous Ghalib couplet, '*Umre bhar Ghalib yahi bhool karta raha, dhool chehre pe thi, aur aina saaf karta raha!* (His whole life, Ghalib kept repeating one mistake, the dust was on his face, but he kept cleaning the mirror!)' And like a video on auto-play I see this same story that Vibha has convinced herself of, repeat itself time and time again on various occasions and in different circumstances.

Our annual sales conference is underway as the new financial year begins, and there is a palpable air of good cheer and optimism all around us. The year gone by has been analysed in great detail and, depending on the sales achievement percentage for the year, either lovingly wrapped in soft cloth like the zari saree mother gave us and put away in the cupboard or unlovingly dumped in old newspaper like a piece of rotting fish and consigned to the dustbin.

But it's a new year and an opportunity to start again with a clean slate, and to add further joy, a Bollywood sports film has just released with tremendous success at the box office, so we have a fresh sales anthem too! A bright and shining new dawn looms on the horizon of sales teams across the length and breadth of the country. Who wouldn't feel all roused and enthusiastic then? Especially if Shah Rukh Khan is personally exhorting everyone to chale-chalo?

As the conference ends, I ask the team, 'Are you comfortable with the targets?' 'YES WE ARE,' they scream. 'Are you confident of achieving them?' 'YES WE ARE,' they roar even more buoyantly. 'Who takes charge of these numbers?' I push further. 'EACH OF US DO!!!' And the conference ends with a victory cry.

Now fast-forward to the mid-year review. It's been a mixed bag in terms of results. Some hits, some misses and a stuttering economy have kept things pretty muted. I ask the sales team about their below-par performance, 'So what happened?' And out pours a litany of reasons, from 'HR didn't give me enough people to work with', to the fact that competition dropped rates to gain share, to the economy that was hit by oil prices and finally, an accusatory finger pointed firmly at climate change. And suddenly the accountability that the team had started the year with unaccountably disappears!

I see this happen all the time, every time. Inevitably people outsource their lives to their circumstances or to other people around them by refusing to take culpability for anything that happens to them. They are essentially admitting that not they, but someone else is responsible for their successes and failures.

The worst consequence of this behaviour is that not only do people never seek to improve their actions in whatever drama that is unfolding, but at some stage they also start feeling powerless to change their own destiny. They believe that their actions can have no discernable and definite impact on their lives and end up relying on externalities for restitution. They become either victims or bystanders of their own lives.

In contrast, the moment we start thinking that we lost the ball, finding it becomes our responsibility, our prerogative, and we automatically start thinking about solutions. We tell ourselves that this quagmire we are embroiled in is a consequence of the decisions we have taken, but that's okay, because we also have the ability and capability to find a way out of it. This is an extremely powerful message to the brain and it is exactly what good leaders do.

Great leaders take control of the destiny of not only their own lives but also the lives of the people and organisations around them. They solve problems and find solutions to the messes other people create and by doing so they become the heroes of the story and of the narrative, which they control. The hero strides into the story and saves the day with her strength, guile and intelligence, completely comfortable in the knowledge that she had the ability to do so from the very start. Meanwhile, the victim wanders about in a lost manner, waiting for one more villain to blame, and the bystander in the story lets others determine what the next course of action will be in her life.

Isn't the distinction between these roles only hinged on taking accountability for everything that happens in the tale? And that's both the beginning and the end of the leadership saga.

Amy Cuddy, a well-known social psychologist, has propagated the use of a bodily action called 'power poses' where a person stands in a powerful stance (such as upright with arms spread out or in the veerabhadra asana, which is the warrior pose in yoga) for a few minutes before any high-pressure task such as an interview or presentation. This is supposed to instil a feeling of self-belief and confidence, which in turn has a positive impact on performance. Similarly, when you're in front of a mirror, make it a point to talk to yourself about how everything that has happened in your life is a result and consequence of your actions and your actions alone. Question the occasions when you let others rule your life for you and then promise yourself that never again will you let it happen, because only you have the final lien on your life. The moment you do that you will see the power flowing within you and the ability to find your own solutions.

As W.E. Henley says in *Invictus*, 'It matters not how strait the gate, how charged with punishments the scroll, I am the master of my fate, I am the captain of my soul.'

And that master and captain is you, dear lady boss. No one else.

IN SHORT

- The ultimate trait of a leader is personal accountability, where she takes complete charge of her destiny and also the destinies of the people around her.
- Externalising problems is a negative emotion. While being a momentary salve, it conveys to the mind a sense of helplessness and failure.
- Only by accepting that we are responsible for both the good and the bad that happens around us will we move into a solution mindset and that feeling of control will help us resolve the issues facing us and our teams.
- We need to consciously work on owning responsibility for our actions and the consequences thereof, so that we can become effective leaders.

Epilogue

What is the measure of your ambition? Would you like to weigh your life against diamonds and pearls and other markers of wealth? Or would you prefer to measure it on a speedometer in terms of the number of activities completed in a day or a month, maybe the number of frequent flier points you collect as you whizz through 265 days of travel every year? Perhaps you would like to assess it in terms of the happiness you gave your family, in the nurturing of two lovely children and the loving care you took of your parents as they aged in front of your eyes? Will the fact that you gave up the rat race for the passion of teaching, travelling or writing be your epitaph? At the time of the final judgement, will you rest your case of being successful on the evidence of having built a fine organisation, or a boutique firm from scratch, or the number of close and lasting friendships you had?

To every one of us is given the choice of what scale we want to gauge our life against, and then decide how well we performed on it. This book is not a guide or lesson on whether the choices you made or the goals you sought were right or wrong, good or bad. I wrote this book to tell you that you and you alone should have the power and authority to make that choice. Without the baggage of expectations, without the affliction of being seen as a woman in a largely male-dominated world, without the conditioning that was injected in your veins and the veins of your mother and grandmother – only you should decide who you are and what you want to become.

And as you stand and look at yourself in the mirror and reclaim your agency to make that choice, this book, as all good catalysts do, tells you what to *stop, start* and *continue* doing.

So stop saying yes when you mean no. It is okay to say maybe too, when you are not sure. Stop being that patient listener of the pompous male voices around you. Stop putting everyone else's needs before yours. Stop jumping up to make the coffee when you are the only woman in the room. Stop rushing to agree with an opinion that you secretly believe is incorrect just for the sake of keeping the peace or because the person opposite has a loud voice or because he sounds far more confident than you do. Stop minimising your achievements and attributing them to luck rather than the hard work you have put in so far. And do stop looking at only your flaws and making them larger than they actually are.

Please continue to be aware that you are different and therein lies your biggest strength and your ability to bring change in the world around you. This realisation has finally dawned upon you a little later than I would have liked, but since we are finally there, celebrate your uniqueness and your ability to see differing points of view, a talent only the very wise have. Enjoy the fact that your nurturing abilities can turn not only your little babies into outstanding adults, but also your employees into great professionals. Look around yourself and see how much the world needs your clarity of thinking, practical good sense and implementation skills to make sense of the chaos we have created and to undo the damage we have wrought on our planet. Look no further than at some of the outstanding women leaders around you who have demonstrated the ability to take tough decisions, the empathy to create bonds with their people and the inspiring vocabulary to align them towards a common charter. You are one of that tribe too. So let out that curly hair from that oiled plait, un-layer that dusky skin from the industrial level coatings of the latest fairness cream and don't worry if you are the only soprano in a room full of baritones and basses. Revel in being different and owning your true self.

To bring about the changes you desire, you cannot continue using the current instruments of trade. Change will only happen if you change the tools, which need to be uniquely yours and different from the ones used thus far. Audre Lorde, the American writer and feminist said, 'The Master's tools will never dismantle the Master's house.' It is an imperative and a necessity to remain different, to not fall in the trap of moulding yourself into becoming one of the boys or the boys' plaything.

Finally, start standing straight and tall, talking loudly and laughing boisterously. The default background score in our public and private spaces is deafeningly male. You need to change that. Your invisibility and your silence have been your biggest weakness. You are wise, you are talented and bright, but you have not been bold and brave. It is time you stood up to be counted. Display your legs and cleavage at your will. And ask the gentleman sitting next to you not to peer down your neckline. If he can stare openly, you can tell him to not do so as openly too. If you disagree with your board members, say so in the boardroom itself and don't hide behind one-on-one chats. Start letting go of your children, the wounds in your past, the organisation that did not give you growth or paid you less than your male colleagues, and even your desire to feel needed or to get married if you don't want to!

You have the entire universe inside you, so why do you allow yourself to be condensed or minimised into a microcosm? As you practise, so will you become. So practise the swagger, practise being flamboyant and confident, practise walking with a sway of your hips, a song on your lips and laughter in your heart. Practise, practise, practise this. Henceforth and more!

And as you reclaim your true position on this planet, remember you are giving strength to other women too. When they watch you, they will learn; and when they learn, they will grow. That is the only way we will quicken the pace of change and begin to hold up half the sky that rightfully belongs to us, one woman holding up one corner of it at a time! The sisterhood coming together, in a shared culture of kindness, nurturing and support is the only way to dismantle the existing patriarchal norms and you cannot let your community down by remaining a passive bystander.

When you unleash the leader in you, I hope this book and the points I am leaving with you to reflect on will help you maximise your real potential in its highest and truest form and give you all that your heart desires, in whichever form or shape you have chosen to bring these yearnings alive.

From one sister to another – may the force be with you!

Acknowledgements

Rakhi Chakraborty and Siddharth Purohit – my research assistants. This book is as much theirs as it is mine.

Deepa Dave, Rachna Kanwar, Tinaz Nooshian, Aparna Vishwasrao, Swapnalekha Basak, Kiran Manral, Kanchan Purohit, Divya Oberoi, Sulekha Bajpai, Sarika Bhattacharyya, Sagorika Kantharia, Monica Chaudhari and all the other gutsy ladies I know, whose stories inspire me every day.

RKA – friend, colleague, thought provocateur and guide. Teachers need someone to teach them too.

Kanishka Gupta from Writer's Side, who wouldn't give up and incessantly kept telling me that I had another book in me.

Varsha Ojha, Priyanka Gupta, Mitali Jathar and Sonia Mansata along with Team Archetype for their passionate and ardent support of my work.

V. Karthika and the entire team at Amazon-Westland for their faith in the book.

Sangeetha Kabadi and Jimmy Oza – life is easier and better with them around.